family circle®

quick
PASTA
recipes

The Family Circle® Promise of Success

Welcome to the world of Confident Cooking,
created for you in the Australian **Family Circle®
Test Kitchen,** where recipes are double-tested by
our team of home economists to achieve a
high standard of success—and delicious
results every time.

MURDOCH
B O O K S

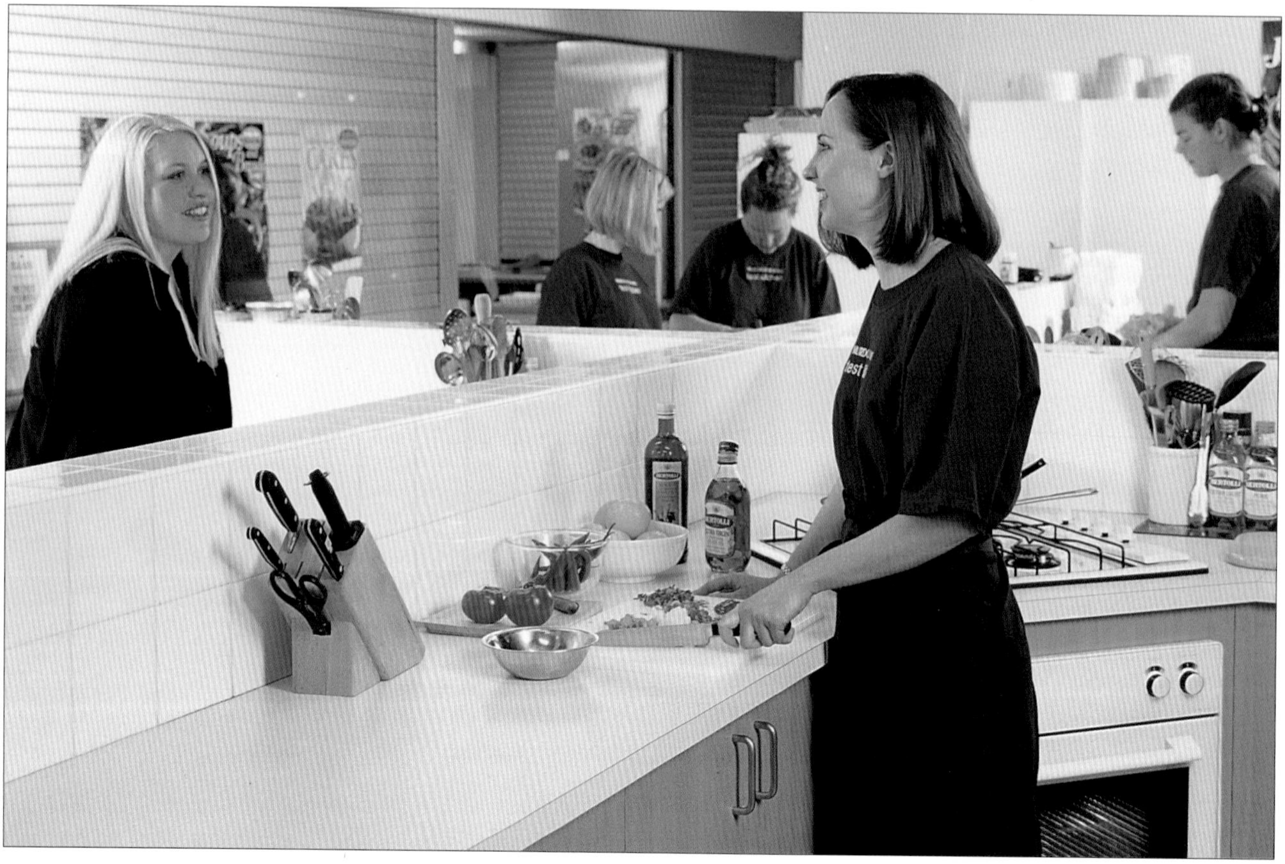

TEST KITCHEN PERFECTION

You'll never make a wrong move with a Family Circle® step-by-step cookbook. Our team of home economists has tested and refined the recipes so that you can create fabulous food in your own kitchen. Follow our easy instructions and step-by-step photographs and you'll feel like there is a master chef in the kitchen guiding you every step of the way.

All recipes are double-tested by our team of home economists. When we test our recipes, we rate them for ease of preparation. The following cookery ratings are on the recipes in this book, making them easy to use and understand.

A single Cooking with Confidence symbol indicates a recipe that is simple and generally quick to make—perfect for beginners.

Two symbols indicate the need for just a little more care and a little more time.

Three symbols indicate special dishes that need more investment in time, care and patience—but the results are worth it.

The Publisher thanks the following for their assistance: Corso De' Fiori, Country Road, Lincraft, Smeg Appliances, Witchery, Chief Australia, Breville Holdings Pty Ltd, Kambrook, Sheldon & Hammond, Bertolli Olive Oil, Southcorp Appliances.

Front cover: Spaghetti with smoked tuna and olives (page 61).
Inside front cover: Cavatelli with pecorino and a herb sauce (page 22).
Back cover: Orecchiette with spiced pumpkin and yoghurt (page 25).

CONTENTS

Top: Veal tortellini with baked pumpkin and basil butter (page 77). *Bottom:* Warm pasta and smoked salmon stack (page 108), Rich cheese macaroni (page 33).

PERFECT PASTA

THROW SOME PASTA INTO A POT OF BOILING WATER AND WHILE IT BUBBLES AWAY, COOK UP A SIMPLE SAUCE AND YOU HAVE A DELICIOUSLY EASY MEAL.

USING THIS BOOK

There are five main shapes of pasta: short, curly, long, filled and flat. For something a little different, we have divided our recipes into chapters that reflect the shape of the pasta they use. The same pasta may go by different names around the world, so, to help you identify the pasta shapes we have used, there is a helpful mini glossary at the start of each chapter. The glossary not only helps identify the different pasta types, but also gives some possible substitutions.

STORING PASTA

Dried pasta can be stored in a cool dry place for months. Fresh pasta must be refrigerated and won't keep for very long, so buy it as you need it. Filled pasta is best bought a day or so before you need it, but some vacuum-packed filled pastas can be kept for up to 3 weeks (check the use-by date). It can be frozen in a single layer between sheets of plastic wrap for up to 3 months but creamy fillings don't freeze well.

MATCHING SAUCE TO PASTA

With up to 300 different pasta shapes, it can be confusing knowing which sauce to serve with which pasta shape. A basic rule to remember is that a chunky pasta is best with a chunky sauce and a thin pasta is best with a thin sauce. Chunky pasta shapes enable you to pick up the sauce with the pasta. Smooth, slender pasta shapes will not hold a chunky sauce but will suit a sauce of olive oil or a fresh tomato sauce. Tiny pasta such as ditalini or stelline are usually used in soups.

HOW MUCH PASTA?

As pasta varies so much in shape, size and type, it is hard to be specific about how much pasta you need per serve. The chart below gives some basic guidelines about how much pasta to provide.

	ENTRÉE	MAIN
Fresh pasta	85 g	140 g
Dried pasta	60 g	115 g
Filled pasta	125 g	150 g

COOKING PASTA

Pasta should be cooked in a large, deep saucepan of water to allow room for expansion and to prevent the pasta pieces from sticking to each other. Allow about 6 litres of water for every 500 g pasta, but never use less than 4 litres even for a small amount of pasta. Filled pasta and large pasta, such as lasagne, will need more water, between 9 and 12 litres, because they are more likely to stick.

If you need to cook large amounts of pasta, only cook up to 1 kg of pasta in one saucepan.

Always bring the water to the boil before stirring in the pasta. When the water comes back to the boil, begin timing, stirring often once the pasta softens a little. Test the pasta just prior to the final cooking time.

Adding oil to the pasta while cooking contributes very little, but seasoning the water with a little salt can add to the flavour. This is entirely a matter of personal preference.

COOKING TIME

Cooking times for pasta vary enormously depending on the size, shape and freshness of the pasta. Generally, the fresher the pasta, the shorter the cooking time. Fresh pasta from a delicatessen or pasta shop usually only needs 1–2 minutes. Vacuum-packed fresh pasta from the supermarket requires a little longer— about 6 minutes. Dried pasta varies depending on the size and shape but because it needs rehydrating as well as cooking, it usually takes longer than fresh pasta. For the most accurate times for all pasta, follow the instructions on the packet.

The best way to ensure pasta is cooked is to taste it. The pasta should be just tender, not at all raw or soft and gluggy. This is referred to in Italian as *al dente* which literally means 'to the tooth'.

SERVING UP

Once the pasta is cooked, it is important to drain it in a colander and then turn it either into a heated dish, the pan with the sauce or back into its cooking pan.

Don't overdrain the pasta: it needs to be a little wet for the sauce to coat it well. Never leave pasta sitting in the colander or it will clump together. A little olive oil or butter tossed through drained pasta will prevent it from sticking together.

Never rinse the pasta unless stated in the recipe: it is usually only rinsed if used in a baked meal or served cold in a salad because the starches released in cooking the pasta help it meld beautifully with the sauce.

Timing is essential when preparing a pasta meal. The sauce should be ready as soon as possible after the pasta is cooked because pasta continues to cook if left to sit around and can become soggy and unappetising.

short

These pasta shapes refuse to be overlooked: their versatility means they can be used in almost any meal. Add your favourite sauce and they stand tall.

PENNE

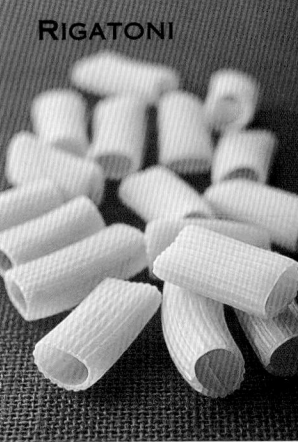

RIGATONI

RISONI

ROTELLE

CAVATELLI: Made from 2–3 cm long pieces of dough that are pressed and pushed with the thumb to make a curved and slightly hollowed oval shape. It is ideal with vegetable sauces, rich tomato sauces and seafood. Replace with orecchiette, pasta gnocchi or sardi (not shown).

CONCHIGLIE (shells): There are three sizes. *Conchiglie* is the most common of the shell pastas and is of a medium size with a ribbed surface that collects a lot of sauce. You can use pasta gnocchi or orecchiette instead. *Conchigliette* is the smallest; usually used in soups. Substitute ditalini or stelline (not shown). *Conchiglione* is the largest and is often stuffed (see page 73 for more information).

DITALINI: One of several tiny pasta shapes that are mainly used in soups, ditalini is a tiny tube-shaped pasta that can either have a smooth or ribbed surface. You can use any of the tiny pastas, such as the little star pasta, stelline (not shown), or orzo.

FARFALLE: The name means butterfly in Italian, which refers to its pretty shape. It is best with thick or chunky sauces, which catch in the folds. You can also use a similar-sized pasta, such as fusilli (page 31) or penne.

MACARONI: Very similar to elbow macaroni (page 31) but without the curve. Macaroni, otherwise known as straight macaroni, is a small tube pasta usually used in soups and bakes. The best substitute is elbow macaroni, but you can also use cotelli or garganelli (page 31).

ORECCHIETTE: Orecchiette means little ears in Italian, and the name of the pasta is a typically literal description of the shape—although some brands look more like curls than ears. It is best with thick or chunky sauces. You can substitute cavatelli, conchiglie or pasta gnocchi.

ORZO: In Italian, orzo means barley and the pasta is so-called because of its similarity in appearance to grains of barley. It is mainly used in clear soups, but it can also be used as a substitute for rice in risotto. It is a little bigger than risoni.

PASTA GNOCCHI: Not to be confused with the potato dumplings of the same name, pasta gnocchi is, as the name suggests, a pasta of a similar shape to potato gnocchi. The curves of the pasta make is especially suitable to being served with thick or chunky sauces. Some suitable replacements are cavatelli, conchiglie or orecchiette.

PENNE: A popular quill-shaped tube, sometimes ribbed and sometimes plain. It is usually about 4 cm long. It is best with thick or chunky sauces. You can replace it with a pasta of a similar size, such as fusilli, garganelli (page 31), passatelli (not shown), or rigatoni.

RIGATONI: There are many sizes of this tube-shaped pasta. The largest size is usually stuffed and baked, but the other sizes are all interchangeable. The ribbed walls of the pasta catch the sauce. You can substitute large fusilli (page 31), penne or rotelle.

RISONI: This is a small pasta that looks very similar to arborio rice. It is best used in soups, bakes and casseroles or when used in a risotto instead of rice. Stelline (not shown), orzo or ditalini will work well in the same recipes (but not in risotto).

ROTELLE: Otherwise known as ruote, this pasta has a very distinctive wheel shape. Traditionally it is served with a tomato sauce, but it is suitable for most sauces. If you need to replace it, use a pasta of similar size, such as cresti di gallo (page 31), farfalle or rigatoni.

WARM CHICKEN AND PASTA SALAD

Preparation time: 15 minutes
Cooking time: 15 minutes
Serves 4

375 g penne
100 ml olive oil
4 slender eggplants, thinly sliced
  on the diagonal
2 chicken breast fillets
2 teaspoons lemon juice
1/2 cup (15 g) chopped fresh
  flat-leaf parsley
270 g chargrilled red capsicum,
  drained and sliced (see Note)
155 g fresh asparagus, trimmed,
  blanched and cut into 5 cm
  lengths
85 g semi-dried tomatoes, finely
  sliced

1 Cook the pasta in a large saucepan of boiling water until *al dente*. Drain, return to the pan and keep warm. Heat 2 tablespoons of the oil in a large frying pan over high heat and cook the eggplant for 4–5 minutes, or until golden and cooked through.
2 Heat a lightly oiled chargrill pan over high heat and cook the chicken for 5 minutes each side, or until browned and cooked through. Cut into thick slices. Combine the lemon juice, parsley and the remaining oil in a small jar and shake well. Return the pasta to the heat, toss through the dressing, chicken, eggplant, capsicum, asparagus and tomato until well mixed and warmed through. Season with black pepper. Serve warm with a scattering of grated Parmesan, if desired.

NUTRITION PER SERVE
Fat 28 g; Protein 50 g; Carbohydrate 71.5 g; Dietary Fibre 7.5 g; Cholesterol 113.5 mg; 3120 kJ (745 Cal)

COOK'S FILE
Note: Jars of chargrilled capsicum can be bought at the supermarket; otherwise, visit your local deli.

RISONI RISOTTO WITH MUSHROOMS AND PANCETTA

Preparation time: 15 minutes
Cooking time: 35 minutes
Serves 4–6

25 g butter
2 cloves garlic, finely chopped
150 g piece pancetta, diced
400 g button mushrooms, sliced
500 g risoni
1 litre chicken stock
1/2 cup (125 ml) cream
1/2 cup (50 g) finely grated Parmesan
4 tablespoons finely chopped fresh
   flat-leaf parsley

1   Melt the butter in a saucepan, add the garlic and cook over medium heat for 30 seconds, then increase the heat to high, add the pancetta and cook for a further 3–5 minutes, or until crisp. Add the mushrooms and cook for 3–5 minutes, or until they have softened.

2   Add the risoni, stir until it is coated in the mixture, then add the stock and bring to the boil. Reduce the heat to medium and cook, covered, for 15–20 minutes, or until nearly all the liquid has evaporated and the risoni is tender.

3   Stir in the cream and cook, uncovered, for a further 3 minutes, stirring occasionally until the cream is absorbed. Stir in 1/3 cup (35 g) of the Parmesan and all the parsley and season to taste with salt and cracked black pepper. Divide among four serving bowls and serve sprinkled with the remaining Parmesan.

NUTRITION PER SERVE (6)
Fat 20 g; Protein 21.5 g; Carbohydrate 59.5 g; Dietary Fibre 4.5 g; Cholesterol 60 mg; 2110 kJ (505 Cal)

1

2

3

GREEK PASTA SALAD

Preparation time: 10 minutes
Cooking time: 45 minutes
Serves 4

4 Roma tomatoes, quartered
1 tablespoon chopped fresh oregano
500 g rigatoni
250 g marinated soft feta
1 red onion, halved and sliced
1 tablespoon capers in salt, rinsed
and patted dry (see Note)
50 ml red wine vinegar
1/2 cup (15 g) chopped fresh flat-leaf
parsley
2 tablespoons ready-made olive
tapenade

1 Preheat the oven to moderate 180°C (350°F/Gas 4). Place the tomatoes, cut-side-up, on a baking tray, sprinkle with 1 teaspoon of the oregano and season with salt and pepper. Roast for 30–40 minutes, or until soft and caramelised.
2 Meanwhile, cook the pasta in a large saucepan of boiling water until *al dente*. Drain the pasta and return to the pan to keep warm.
3 Drain and crumble the feta, reserving the oil and herbs. Heat 2 teaspoons of the reserved oil in a small frying pan, add the onion and cook over medium heat for 2–3 minutes, or until soft, then add the capers and cook for a further minute. Combine the rest of the reserved oil with the vinegar and stir into the pan. Remove from the heat and stir through the pasta, adding the remaining oregano and the parsley. Divide among four serving plates and top with the tomato, feta and the tapenade.

NUTRITION PER SERVE
Fat 16 g; Protein 26.5 g; Carbohydrate 89 g; Dietary Fibre 6 g; Cholesterol 43 mg; 2570 kJ (615 Cal)

COOK'S FILE
Note: You can buy capers in salt from delicatessens—they are smaller than normal capers and are kept in salt rather than brine. If you want to use capers in brine, buy baby capers and drain them before use.

PASTA GNOCCHI WITH SAUSAGE AND TOMATO

Preparation time: 15 minutes
Cooking time: 20 minutes
Serves 4–6

500 g pasta gnocchi
2 tablespoons olive oil
400 g thin Italian sausages
1 red onion, finely chopped
2 cloves garlic, finely chopped
2 x 415 g cans chopped tomatoes
1 teaspoon caster sugar
35 g fresh basil, torn
1/2 cup (45 g) grated pecorino cheese

1　Cook the pasta in a large saucepan of boiling water until *al dente*. Drain and return the pasta to the pan. Meanwhile, heat 2 teaspoons of the oil in a large frying pan. Add the sausages and cook, turning, for 5 minutes, or until well browned and cooked through. Drain on paper towels, then slice when they have cooled enough to touch. Keep warm.

2　Wipe clean the frying pan and heat the remaining oil. Add the onion and garlic and cook over medium heat for 2 minutes, or until the onion has softened. Add the tomato, sugar and 1 cup (250 ml) water and season well with cracked black pepper. Reduce the heat and simmer for 12 minutes, or until thickened and reduced a little.

3　Pour the sauce over the cooked pasta and stir through the sausage, then the basil and half of the cheese. Divide among serving plates and serve hot with the remaining cheese sprinkled over the top.

NUTRITION PER SERVE (6)
Fat 29.5 g; Protein 17 g; Carbohydrate 29.5 g; Dietary Fibre 4 g; Cholesterol 57.5 mg; 1905 kJ (455 Cal)

1

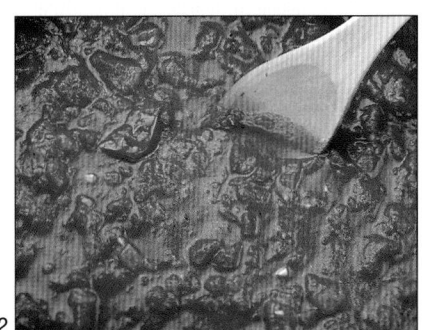

2

3

ROASTED ORANGE SWEET POTATO AND DITALINI PATTIES

Preparation time: 15 minutes
Cooking time: 1 hour 10 minutes
Serves 4

2 orange sweet potatoes
    (about 800 g in total)
1/2 cup (90 g) ditalini
30 g toasted pine nuts
2 cloves garlic, crushed
4 tablespoons finely chopped
    fresh basil
1/2 cup (50 g) grated Parmesan
1/3 cup (35 g) dry breadcrumbs
plain flour, for dusting
olive oil, for shallow-frying

1   Preheat the oven to very hot 250°C (500°F/Gas 10). Pierce the whole orange sweet potatoes several times with a fork, then place in a roasting tin and roast for about 1 hour, or until soft. Remove from the oven and cool. Meanwhile, cook the pasta in a large saucepan of boiling water until *al dente*. Drain and rinse under running water.

2   Peel the sweet potato and mash the flesh with a potato masher or fork, then add the pine nuts, garlic, basil, Parmesan, breadcrumbs and the pasta and combine. Season.

3   Shape the mixture into eight even patties (about 1.5 cm thick) with floured hands, then lightly dust the patties with flour. Heat the oil in a large frying pan and cook the patties in batches over medium heat for 2 minutes each side, or until golden and heated through. Drain on crumpled paper towels, sprinkle with salt and serve immediately. Great with a fresh green salad.

NUTRITION PER SERVE
Fat 15 g; Protein 13.5 g; Carbohydrate 51 g; Dietary Fibre 5.5 g; Cholesterol 12 mg; 1650 kJ (395 Cal)

COOK'S FILE
Note: To save time, drop spoonfuls of the mixture into the pan and flatten with an oiled spatula.
Serving suggestion: The patties are great with aïoli—mix 1 clove of crushed garlic into 1/3 cup (90 g) good-quality whole-egg mayonnaise with a squeeze of lemon juice and season.

TOMATO DITALINI SOUP

Preparation time: 15 minutes
Cooking time: 20 minutes
Serves 4

2 tablespoons olive oil
1 large onion, finely chopped
2 celery sticks, finely chopped
3 vine-ripened tomatoes
1.5 litres chicken or vegetable stock
1/2 cup (90 g) ditalini
2 tablespoons chopped fresh
   flat-leaf parsley

1 Heat the oil in a large saucepan over medium heat. Add the onion and celery and cook for 5 minutes, or until they have softened.

2 Score a cross in the base of each tomato, then place them in a bowl of boiling water for 1 minute. Plunge into cold water and peel the skin away from the cross. Halve the tomatoes and scoop out the seeds. Roughly chop the flesh. Add the stock and tomato to the onion mixture and bring to the boil. Add the pasta and cook for 10 minutes, or until *al dente*. Season and sprinkle with parsley. Serve with crusty bread.

NUTRITION PER SERVE
Fat 11 g; Protein 8 g; Carbohydrate 23 g;
Dietary Fibre 3.5 g; Cholesterol 0 mg;
925 kJ (220 Cal)

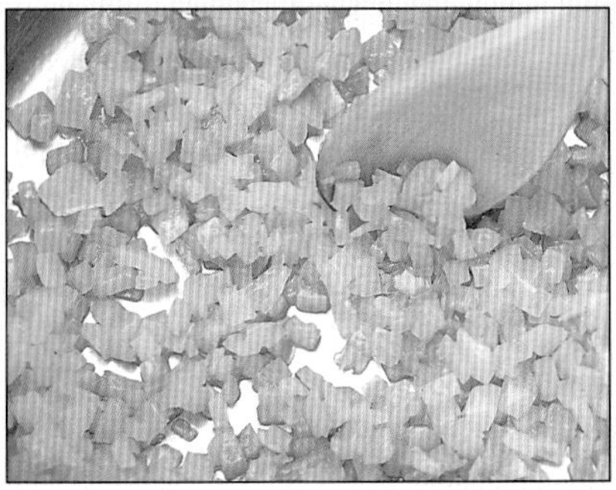

PASTA DI STALLA
(Pasta from the barn)

Preparation time: 10 minutes
Cooking time: 15 minutes
Serves 4

375 g orecchiette
1 large potato, cut into 1.5 cm cubes
400 g broccoli
1/3 cup (80 ml) olive oil
3 cloves garlic, crushed
1 small fresh red chilli, finely chopped
2 x 400 g cans diced tomatoes
1/4 cup (25 g) grated pecorino cheese

1 Bring a large saucepan of salted water to the boil and cook the pasta and potato for 8–10 minutes, or until the pasta is *al dente*. Drain and return to the saucepan. Meanwhile, trim the broccoli into florets and discard the stems. Place in a saucepan of boiling water and cook for 1–2 minutes, then drain and plunge into iced water. Drain and add to the cooked pasta and potato.

2 Heat the oil in a saucepan, add the garlic and chilli and cook for 30 seconds. Add the tomato and simmer for 5 minutes, or until slightly reduced and thickened. Season to taste with salt and cracked black pepper.

3 Pour the tomato mixture over the pasta, potato and broccoli. Toss well and stir over low heat until warmed through. Serve sprinkled with grated pecorino cheese.

NUTRITION PER SERVE
Fat 21.5 g; Protein 19.5 g; Carbohydrate 76.5 g; Dietary Fibre 10.5 g; Cholesterol 5.5 mg; 2445 kJ (585 Cal)

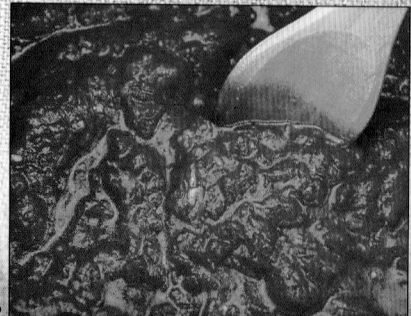

1

2

3

PENNE WITH PUMPKIN, BAKED RICOTTA AND PROSCIUTTO

Preparation time: 15 minutes
Cooking time: 15 minutes
Serves 4

500 g penne
460 g butternut pumpkin, cut into
    1 cm cubes
1/4 cup (60 ml) extra virgin olive oil

2 cloves garlic, crushed
100 g semi-dried tomatoes, chopped
4 slices prosciutto, chopped
250 g baked ricotta, cut into 1 cm
    cubes
3 tablespoons shredded fresh basil

1 Cook the pasta in a large saucepan of boiling water until *al dente*. Drain. Meanwhile, cook the pumpkin in a saucepan of boiling water for 10–12 minutes, or until just tender, then drain.

2 Heat the oil in a large saucepan, add the garlic and cook over medium heat for 30 seconds. Add the tomato, prosciutto, pumpkin and penne and toss gently over low heat for 1–2 minutes, or until heated through.

3 Add the baked ricotta and the basil, season with salt and cracked black pepper and serve immediately.

NUTRITION PER SERVE
Fat 23 g; Protein 28.5 g; Carbohydrate 99 g; Dietary Fibre 8.5 g; Cholesterol 37 mg; 3020 kJ (720 Cal)

1

2

3

CONCHIGLIETTE WITH WALNUT PESTO

Preparation time: 15 minutes
Cooking time: 15 minutes
Serves 4–6

125 g day-old crusty bread, crusts removed
1½ cups (185 g) walnut pieces
500 g conchigliette
½ cup (30 g) firmly packed fresh basil, roughly chopped
2–3 cloves garlic, peeled
1 small fresh red chilli, seeded and roughly chopped
½ teaspoon finely grated lemon rind
¼ cup (60 ml) lemon juice
½ cup (125 ml) olive oil

1 Preheat the oven to warm 160°C (315°F/Gas 2–3). Cut the bread into 2 cm thick slices and place on a baking tray with the walnuts. Bake for 8–10 minutes, or until the bread is dried out a little and the walnuts are lightly toasted. Don't overcook the walnuts or they will be bitter.

2 Meanwhile, cook the pasta in a large saucepan of boiling water until *al dente*. Drain and return the pasta to the pan.

3 Break the bread into chunks and place in the bowl of a food processor. Add the walnuts, basil, garlic, chilli, lemon rind and juice. Use the pulse button to chop the mixture without forming a paste. Transfer to a bowl and stir in the oil. Toss the walnut mixture through the pasta, then season to taste with salt and pepper.

NUTRITION PER SERVE (6)
Fat 38.5 g; Protein 15 g; Carbohydrate 69.5 g; Dietary Fibre 7 g; Cholesterol 0 mg; 2870 kJ (685 Cal)

COOK'S FILE
Note: Don't add the oil to the food processor or the pesto will lose its crunchy texture.

FARFALLE WITH SPINACH AND BACON

Preparation time: 10 minutes
Cooking time: 15 minutes
Serves 4

400 g farfalle
2 tablespoons extra virgin olive oil
250 g bacon, chopped
1 red onion, finely chopped
250 g baby spinach leaves, stalks
 trimmed
1–2 tablespoons sweet chilli sauce
 (optional)
1/4 cup (35 g) crumbled goat's feta

1 Cook the pasta in a large saucepan of boiling water until *al dente*, then drain and return to the saucepan. Meanwhile, heat the oil in a frying pan, add the bacon and cook over medium heat for 3 minutes, or until golden. Add the onion and cook for a further 4 minutes, or until softened. Toss the spinach leaves through the onion and bacon mixture for 30 seconds, or until just wilted.

2 Add the bacon and spinach mixture to the drained pasta, then stir in the sweet chilli sauce. Season to taste with salt and cracked black pepper and toss well. Spoon into warm bowls and scatter with the crumbled feta. Serve immediately.

NUTRITION PER SERVE
Fat 19 g; Protein 28 g; Carbohydrate 73 g;
Dietary Fibre 7 g; Cholesterol 42 mg;
2415 kJ (575 Cal)

1

2

RICOTTA, EGGPLANT AND PASTA TIMBALES

Preparation time: 15 minutes
Cooking time: 45 minutes
Makes 4

1/2 cup (125 ml) light olive oil
1 large eggplant, sliced lengthways into 1 cm slices
200 g straight macaroni
1 small onion, finely chopped
2 cloves garlic, crushed
400 g can diced tomatoes
400 g ricotta
1 cup (80 g) coarsely grated Parmesan
1/2 cup (15 g) shredded fresh basil, plus extra to garnish

1 Preheat the oven to moderate 180°C (350°F/Gas 4). Heat 2 tablespoons of the oil in a large, non-stick frying pan and cook the eggplant in three batches over medium heat for 2–3 minutes each side, or until golden, adding 2 tablespoons of the oil with each batch. Remove from the pan and drain on crumpled paper towels. Meanwhile, cook the pasta in a large saucepan of boiling water until *al dente*. Drain and set aside.

2 Add the onion and garlic to the frying pan and cook over medium heat for 2–3 minutes, or until just golden. Add the tomato and cook for 5 minutes, or until the sauce is pulpy and most of the liquid has evaporated. Season, then remove from the heat.

3 Combine the ricotta, Parmesan and basil in a large bowl, then mix in the pasta. Line the base and sides of four 1 1/2 cup (375 ml) ramekins with eggplant, trimming any overhanging pieces. Top with half the pasta mix, pressing down firmly. Spoon on the tomato sauce, then cover with the remaining pasta mix. Bake for 10–15 minutes, or until heated through and golden on top. Stand for 5 minutes, then run a knife around the ramekin to loosen the timbale. Invert onto plates, garnish with a sprig of basil and serve with a side salad and crusty bread.

NUTRITION PER TIMBALE
Fat 40 g; Protein 25.5 g; Carbohydrate 42.5 g; Dietary Fibre 6 g; Cholesterol 67 mg; 2645 kJ (630 Cal)

1

2

3

CREAMY PASTA GNOCCHI WITH PEAS AND PROSCIUTTO

Preparation time: 15 minutes
Cooking time: 20 minutes
Serves 4

100 g thinly sliced prosciutto
3 teaspoons oil
2 eggs
1 cup (250 ml) cream
1/3 cup (35 g) finely grated Parmesan
2 tablespoons chopped fresh flat-leaf parsley
1 tablespoon chopped fresh chives
250 g fresh or frozen peas
500 g pasta gnocchi

1 Cut the prosciutto into 5 mm wide strips. Heat the oil in a frying pan over medium heat, add the prosciutto and cook for 2 minutes, or until crisp. Drain on paper towels. Place the eggs, cream, Parmesan and herbs in a bowl and whisk well.
2 Bring a large saucepan of salted water to the boil. Add the peas and cook for 5 minutes, or until just tender. Leaving the pan on the heat, use a slotted spoon and transfer the peas to the bowl of cream mixture, and then add 1/4 cup (60 ml) of the cooking liquid to the same bowl. Using a potato masher or the back of a fork, roughly mash the peas.
3 Add the gnocchi to the boiling water and cook until *al dente*. Drain well, then return to the pan. Add the cream mixture, then warm through over low heat, gently stirring for about 30 seconds until the gnocchi is coated in the sauce. Season to taste with salt and cracked black pepper. Divide among warmed plates, top with the prosciutto and serve immediately.

NUTRITION PER SERVE
Fat 32.5 g; Protein 21 g; Carbohydrate 41 g; Dietary Fibre 6 g; Cholesterol 201 mg; 2260 kJ (540 Cal)

COOK'S FILE
Note: Be careful not to overheat or cook for too long as the egg will begin to set and the result will look like a scrambled egg sauce.

PASTA E FAGIOLI
(Hearty pasta and bean soup)

Preparation time: 15 minutes
Cooking time: 20 minutes
Serves 4

1 tablespoon olive oil
1 onion, finely chopped
3 cloves garlic, crushed
2 x 290 g cans mixed beans, drained
1.75 litres chicken stock (see Note)
100 g conchigliette
1 tablespoon chopped fresh tarragon

1 Heat the oil in a saucepan over low heat. Add the onion and cook for 5 minutes, then add the garlic and cook for a further 1 minute, stirring frequently. Add the beans and chicken stock, cover the pan with a lid, increase the heat and bring to the boil. Add the pasta and cook until *al dente*. Stir in the tarragon, then season with salt and cracked black pepper. Serve with crusty bread.

1

NUTRITION PER SERVE
Fat 6.5 g; Protein 12 g; Carbohydrate 34 g; Dietary Fibre 8 g; Cholesterol 0 mg; 1015 kJ (240 Cal)

COOK'S FILE
Note: The flavour of this soup is really enhanced by using a good-quality stock. Either make your own or use the tetra packs of liquid stock that are available at the supermarket.

ZUCCHINI PASTA BAKE

Preparation time: 15 minutes
Cooking time: 40 minutes
Serves 4

200 g risoni
40 g butter
4 spring onions, thinly sliced
400 g zucchini, grated
4 eggs
1/2 cup (125 ml) cream
100 g ricotta (see Note)
2/3 cup (100 g) grated mozzarella
3/4 cup (75 g) grated Parmesan

1 Preheat the oven to moderate 180°C (350°F/Gas 4). Cook the pasta in a large saucepan of boiling water until *al dente*. Drain well. Meanwhile, heat the butter in a frying pan, add the spring onion and cook for 1 minute, then add the zucchini and cook for a further 4 minutes, or until soft. Cool slightly.

2 Place the eggs, cream, ricotta, mozzarella, risoni and half of the Parmesan in a bowl and mix together well. Stir in the zucchini mixture, then season with salt and pepper. Spoon the mixture into four 2 cup (500 ml) greased ovenproof dishes, but do not fill to the brim. Sprinkle with the remaining Parmesan and cook for 25–30 minutes, or until firm and golden.

NUTRITION PER SERVE
Fat 40.5 g; Protein 28.5 g; Carbohydrate 39 g; Dietary Fibre 4.5 g; Cholesterol 310.5 mg; 2635 kJ (630 Cal)

COOK'S FILE
Note: With such simple flavours, it is important to use good-quality fresh ricotta from the delicatessen or the deli section of your local supermarket.

CAVATELLI WITH PECORINO AND A HERB SAUCE

Preparation time: 10 minutes
Cooking time: 15 minutes
Serves 4

400 g cavatelli
80 g butter
2 cloves garlic, crushed
3 tablespoons chopped fresh chives
3 tablespoons shredded fresh basil
1 tablespoon shredded fresh sage
1 teaspoon fresh thyme
1/4 cup (60 ml) warm vegetable stock
2/3 cup (60 g) firmly packed grated
    pecorino cheese

1 Cook the pasta in a large saucepan of boiling water until *al dente*. Meanwhile, heat the butter in a small saucepan over medium heat, add the garlic and cook for 1 minute, or until fragrant. Add the chives, basil, sage and thyme and cook for a further minute.

2 Drain the pasta and return to the pan. Add the herb mixture and stock. Return to the heat for 2–3 minutes, or until warmed through. Season to taste with salt and cracked black pepper. Add the grated pecorino and stir until well combined. Divide among four warm serving bowls and garnish with sage leaves, if desired.

NUTRITION PER SERVE
Fat 21.5 g; Protein 16 g; Carbohydrate 71 g; Dietary Fibre 5.5 g; Cholesterol 64.5 mg; 2280 kJ (545 Cal)

COOK'S FILE
Note: Pecorino is sheep's milk cheese with a sharp flavour. If unavailable, use Parmesan instead.

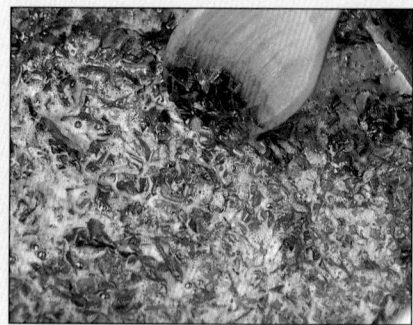

PENNE WITH VEAL RAGOUT

Preparation time: 15 minutes
Cooking time: 2 hours 40 minutes
Serves 4

2 onions, sliced
2 bay leaves, crushed
1.5 kg veal shin, cut into osso buco
pieces (see Note)
1 cup (250 ml) red wine
2 x 400 g cans crushed tomatoes
1½ cups (375 ml) beef stock
2 teaspoons chopped fresh rosemary
400 g penne
1 cup (140 g) frozen peas

1 Preheat the oven to hot 220°C (425°F/Gas 7). Scatter the onion over the bottom of a large roasting tin (we used 32 x 23 cm), lightly spray with oil and place the bay leaves and veal pieces on top. Season with salt and pepper. Roast for 10–15 minutes, or until the veal is browned. Watch the onion to make sure that it doesn't burn.

2 Pour the wine over the veal and return to the oven for a further 5 minutes. Reduce the heat to moderate 180°C (350°F/Gas 4), remove the tin from the oven and pour on the tomato, stock and 1 teaspoon of the rosemary. Cover with foil and return to the oven. Cook for 2 hours, or until the veal is starting to fall from the bone. Remove the foil and cook for a further 15 minutes, or until the meat loosens away from the bone and the liquid has evaporated slightly.

3 Cook the pasta in a large saucepan of boiling water until *al dente*. Meanwhile, remove the veal from the oven and cool slightly. Add the peas and remaining rosemary and place over a hotplate. Cook over medium heat for 5 minutes, or until the peas are cooked. Drain the pasta, divide among four bowls and top with the ragout.

NUTRITION PER SERVE
Fat 5 g; Protein 51.5 g; Carbohydrate 81 g;
Dietary Fibre 10 g; Cholesterol 125 mg;
2605 kJ (620 Cal)

COOK'S FILE
Notes: Most butchers sell veal shin cut into osso buco pieces. If sold in a whole piece, ask the butcher to cut it for you (the pieces are about 3–4 cm thick). It is also available at some supermarkets. You can either remove the meat from the bone before serving, or leave it on.

1

2

3

CAJUN SCALLOPS, CONCHIGLIETTE AND BUTTERY CORN SAUCE

Preparation time: 15 minutes
Cooking time: 15 minutes
Serves 4

350 g conchigliette or conchiglie
20 large scallops, without roe
2 tablespoons Cajun spice mix
2 tablespoons corn oil
250 g butter
3 cloves garlic, crushed
400 g can corn kernels, drained
1/4 cup (60 ml) lime juice
4 tablespoons finely chopped fresh
   coriander leaves

1 Cook the pasta in a large saucepan of boiling water until *al dente*. Drain and return to the pan to keep warm. Meanwhile, pat the scallops dry with paper towel and lightly coat in the spice mix. Heat the oil in a large frying pan and cook the scallops for 1 minute each side over high heat (ensuring they are well spaced), then remove from the pan, cover and keep warm.
2 Reduce the heat to medium, add the butter and cook for 4 minutes, or until foaming and golden brown. Remove from the heat, add the garlic, corn and lime juice. Gently toss the corn mixture through the pasta with 2 tablespoons of the coriander and season well. Divide among four serving plates, top with the scallops,

drizzle with any juices and sprinkle with the remaining coriander.

NUTRITION PER SERVE
Fat 60.5 g; Protein 20 g; Carbohydrate 75 g; Dietary Fibre 7 g; Cholesterol 174.5 mg; 3850 kJ (920 Cal)

COOK'S FILE
Notes: Scallops should not be crowded when they are cooked or they will release all their juices, causing the scallops to stew and become tough. Use a good-quality Cajun spice mix as this will affect the flavour of the dish. To really achieve the most delicious flavours, don't use a non-stick frying pan—they can prevent the butter from properly browning and the juices from caramelising.

1

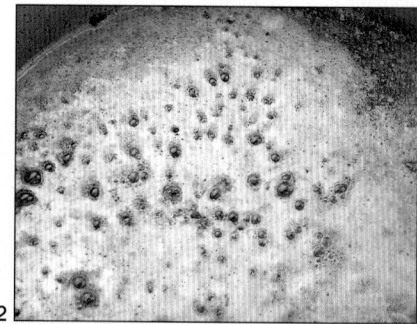

2

ORECCHIETTE WITH SPICED PUMPKIN AND YOGHURT

Preparation time: 15 minutes
Cooking time: 35 minutes
Serves 6

1 kg pumpkin, cut into 2 cm cubes
1/3 cup (80 ml) olive oil
500 g orecchiette
2 cloves garlic, crushed
1 teaspoon dried chilli flakes
1 teaspoon coriander seeds, crushed
1 tablespoon cumin seeds, crushed
200 g Greek-style natural yoghurt
3 tablespoons chopped fresh
   coriander leaves

1 Preheat the oven to moderately hot 200°C (400°F/Gas 6). Toss the pumpkin in 2 tablespoons of the oil, place in a roasting tin and cook for 30 minutes, or until golden and crisp, tossing halfway through.

2 Meanwhile, cook the pasta in a large saucepan of boiling water until *al dente*. Drain, then return to the saucepan.

3 Heat the remaining oil in a saucepan. Add the garlic, chilli, coriander and cumin and cook for 30 seconds, or until fragrant. Toss the spice mix and pumpkin through the pasta, then stir in the yoghurt and fresh coriander and season to taste with salt and cracked black pepper. Divide among serving bowls and serve.

NUTRITION PER SERVE
Fat 15 g; Protein 14.5 g; Carbohydrate 71.5 g; Dietary Fibre 6.5 g; Cholesterol 5.5 mg; 2035 kJ (485 Cal)

1

2

3

ROTELLE WITH CHICKPEAS, TOMATO AND PARSLEY

Preparation time: 10 minutes
Cooking time: 15 minutes
Serves 4

375 g rotelle
1 tablespoon ground cumin
1/2 cup (125 ml) olive oil
1 red onion, halved and thinly sliced
3 cloves garlic, crushed
400 g can chickpeas, drained
3 large tomatoes, diced
1/2 cup (15 g) chopped fresh
    flat-leaf parsley
1/4 cup (60 ml) lemon juice

1 Cook the pasta in a large saucepan of boiling water until *al dente*. Drain and return to the pan.

2 Meanwhile, heat a large frying pan over medium heat, add the cumin and cook, tossing, for 1 minute, or until fragrant. Remove from the pan. Heat half the oil in the same pan and cook the onion over medium heat for 2–3 minutes, or until soft. Stir in the garlic, chickpeas, tomato and parsley and stir until warmed through. Gently toss through the pasta.

3 Place the lemon juice, cumin and remaining oil in a jar with a lid and shake together well. Add the dressing to the saucepan with the pasta and chickpea mixture, return to the stove-top over low heat and stir until warmed through. Season well with salt and cracked black pepper. Serve hot with grated Parmesan, or you can serve it cold. If serving cold, rinse the pasta under cold water before adding the chickpea mixture and do not return to the heat.

NUTRITION PER SERVE
Fat 27 g; Protein 17 g; Carbohydrate 80 g; Dietary Fibre 10 g; Cholesterol 0 mg; 2655 kJ (635 Cal)

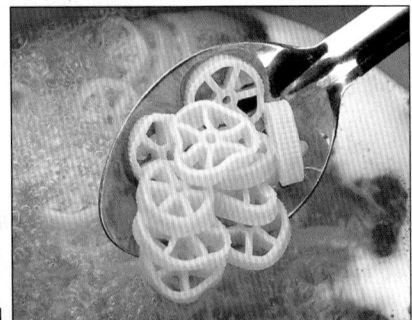
1

2

3

PENNE WITH RUSTIC LENTIL SAUCE

Preparation time: 10 minutes
Cooking time: 30 minutes
Serves 4

1 litre chicken stock
350 g penne
1/3 cup (80 ml) virgin olive oil,
    plus extra for drizzling
1 onion, chopped
2 carrots, diced
3 celery sticks, diced
3 cloves garlic, crushed
1 tablespoon plus 1 teaspoon
    chopped fresh thyme
400 g can lentils, drained

1 Boil the chicken stock in a large saucepan for 10 minutes, or until reduced to 2 cups (500 ml) of liquid. Meanwhile, cook the pasta in a large saucepan of boiling water until *al dente*. Drain and toss with 2 tablespoons of the olive oil.

2 Heat the remaining oil in a large, deep frying pan, add the onion, carrot and celery and cook over medium heat for 10 minutes, or until browned. Add two thirds of the crushed garlic and 1 tablespoon of the thyme and cook for a further 1 minute. Add the stock, bring to the boil and cook for 8 minutes, or until reduced slightly and the vegetables are tender. Gently stir in the lentils until heated through.

3 Stir in the remaining garlic and thyme, and season with plenty of salt and cracked black pepper—the stock should be slightly syrupy at this point. Combine the pasta with the lentil sauce in a large bowl, drizzle generously with virgin olive oil and serve with grated Parmesan, if desired.

NUTRITION PER SERVE
Fat 18 g; Protein 16.5 g; Carbohydrate 72 g; Dietary Fibre 9 g; Cholesterol 0 mg; 2165 kJ (515 Cal)

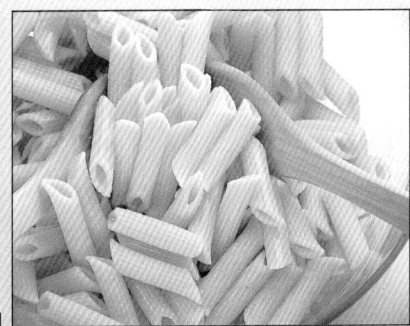

ORZO AND GREEK CHEESE BAKE

Preparation time: 15 minutes
Cooking time: 40 minutes
Serves 6

2 cups (415 g) orzo
60 g butter
6 spring onions, chopped
450 g English spinach, stems
   removed, rinsed well and chopped
2 tablespoons plain flour
1.25 litres milk
250 g kefalotyri cheese, grated
   (see Note)
250 g marinated feta, well drained
3 tablespoons chopped fresh dill

1 Preheat the oven to moderately hot 190°C (375°F/Gas 5). Cook the pasta in a large saucepan of boiling water until *al dente*. Drain well, then return to the pan. Heat 20 g of the butter in a large saucepan over high heat and cook the spring onion for 30 seconds. Add the spinach and stir for 1 minute, or until wilted. Season and stir into the orzo.

2 Put the remaining butter in the saucepan in which the spinach was cooked. Melt over low heat, then stir in the flour and cook for 1 minute, or until pale and foaming. Remove from the heat and gradually stir in the milk. Return to the heat and stir constantly for 5 minutes, or until the sauce boils and thickens. Add two thirds of the kefalotyri and all of the feta and stir for 2 minutes until melted and well mixed. Remove from the heat and stir in the dill.

3 Combine the pasta mixture with the cheese sauce, season to taste and pour into a lightly greased 2.5 litre ovenproof ceramic dish. Sprinkle the remaining cheese on top and bake for 15 minutes, or until golden. Serve with bread and a salad, if desired.

NUTRITION PER SERVE
Fat 34 g; Protein 30.5 g; Carbohydrate 63 g; Dietary Fibre 6 g; Cholesterol 102.5 mg; 2835 kJ (680 Cal)

COOK'S FILE
Note: Kefalotyri is a hard Greek sheep's milk cheese; it is similar to Parmesan.

ORECCHIETTE WITH BROCCOLI, ANCHOVIES AND BASIL

Preparation time: 15 minutes
Cooking time: 25 minutes
Serves 4–6

600 g broccoli, cut into florets
500 g orecchiette
1 tablespoon olive oil
4 cloves garlic, finely chopped
8 anchovy fillets, roughly chopped
1 cup (250 ml) cream
1 cup (30 g) fresh basil, torn
2 teaspoons finely grated lemon
    rind
100 g grated Parmesan

1 Blanch the broccoli in a large saucepan of boiling salted water for 3–4 minutes. Remove and plunge into chilled water. Drain well with a slotted spoon. Bring the water back to the boil and cook the pasta until *al dente*. Drain, reserving 2 tablespoons of the cooking water.
2 Meanwhile, heat the oil in a frying pan. Add the garlic and anchovies and cook over medium heat for 1–2 minutes, or until the garlic begins to turn golden. Add the broccoli and cook for a further 5 minutes. Add the cream and half the basil and cook for 10 minutes, or until the cream has reduced and slightly thickened and the broccoli is very tender.

3 Purée half the mixture in a food processor until nearly smooth, then return to the pan with the lemon rind, half the Parmesan and 2 tablespoons of the reserved water. Stir together well, then season with salt and cracked black pepper. Add the warm pasta and remaining basil, and toss until well combined. Sprinkle with the remaining Parmesan and serve immediately.

NUTRITION PER SERVE (6)
Fat 28 g; Protein 22.5 g; Carbohydrate 60.5 g; Dietary Fibre 9 g; Cholesterol 76.5 mg; 2455 kJ (585 Cal)

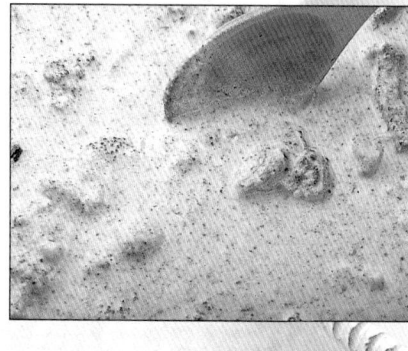

COTELLI

CRESTI DI GALLO

ELBOW MACARONI

FRICELLI

FUSILLI

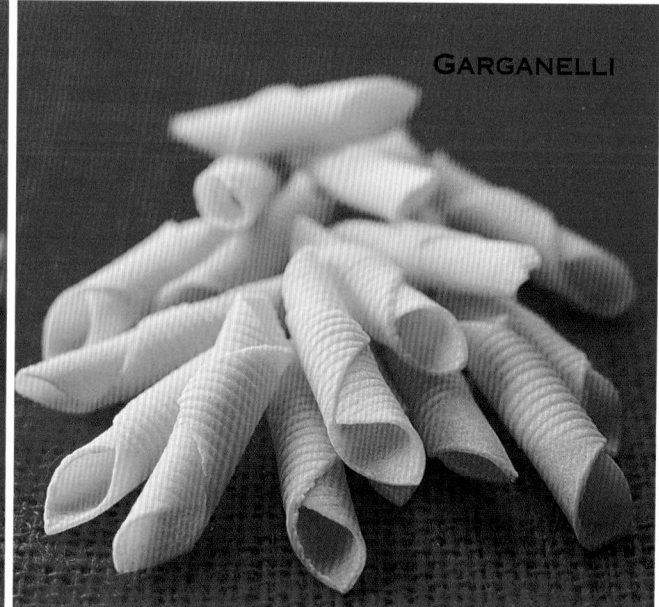

GARGANELLI

curly

The curls and swirls of curly pasta
shapes add interest to even the simplest of sauces.
The challenge is catching them with your fork!

COTELLI: Otherwise known as cavatappi, these hollow tubes of pasta are formed into curls or ringlets. Cotelli is best with thick or chunky sauces as the chunks of the sauce get caught up in the curls. You can substitute a similar-sized and shaped pasta, such as cresti di gallo, elbow macaroni or fusilli.

CRESTI DI GALLO: Named after the Italian word for 'cockscombs', the name of this pasta is a reference to the similarity in shape to the crest of a rooster. Its basic structure is similar to elbow macaroni with the addition of a ruffled frill on the outside edge of the pasta. It can be replaced by rotelle (page 7) or cotelli.

ELBOW MACARONI: The name elbow macaroni is an American term for short curved hollow tubes of pasta. It is part of the macaroni family, with a curve in the middle. Elbow macaroni is usually eaten with sauces based on meat, sausages and tomato. The closest substitutes for elbow macaroni are straight macaroni (page 7), cotelli or garganelli.

FRICELLI: These small tubes of pasta are formed into pretty spirals. They are not always readily available, but you can substitute cavatelli, penne (page 7), fusilli or garganelli.

FUSILLI: This corkscrew-shaped pasta can range in size from 4 to 30 cm long; we have used pieces that are about 4 cm. Fusilli is most often available in dried form. It is commonly served with meat dishes and simple tomato sauces. You can replace fusilli with farfalle, penne (page 7), cotelli or garganelli.

GARGANELLI: This pasta is made with an egg dough that has grated Parmesan and nutmeg added to it. The outside surface of garganelli is ribbed. The ribs are formed by cutting the pasta into 4 cm squares, wrapping the squares around a conical tool, then pressing them onto a ribbed wooden block. Garganelli is commonly served in a broth or with Bolognese sauce but is suitable for a wide range of pasta sauces. Penne (page 7), fricelli or fusilli can all be substituted for garganelli.

COTELLI WITH SPRING VEGETABLES

Preparation time: 15 minutes
Cooking time: 20 minutes
Serves 4

500 g cotelli
2 cups (310 g) frozen peas
2 cups (310 g) frozen broad beans, blanched and peeled
1/3 cup (80 ml) olive oil
6 spring onions, cut into 3 cm pieces
2 cloves garlic, finely chopped
1 cup (250 ml) chicken stock
12 thin fresh asparagus spears, cut into 5 cm lengths
1 lemon

1 Cook the pasta in a large saucepan of boiling water until *al dente*. Drain, then return to the pan. Meanwhile, place the peas in a saucepan of boiling water and cook them for 1–2 minutes, or until tender. Remove with a slotted spoon and plunge into cold water. Add the broad beans to the same saucepan of boiling water and cook for 1–2 minutes, then drain and plunge into cold water. Remove and slip the skins off.

2 Heat 2 tablespoons of the oil in a frying pan. Add the spring onion and garlic and cook over medium heat for 2 minutes, or until softened. Pour in the stock and cook for 5 minutes, or until slightly reduced. Add the asparagus and cook for 3–4 minutes, or until bright green and just tender. Stir in the peas and broad beans and cook for 2–3 minutes, or until heated through.

3 Toss the remaining oil through the pasta, then add the vegetable mixture, 1/2 teaspoon finely grated lemon rind and 1/4 cup (60 ml) lemon juice. Season to taste with salt and cracked black pepper and toss together well. Divide among four bowls and top with shaved Parmesan, if desired.

NUTRITION PER SERVE
Fat 20.5 g; Protein 24.5 g; Carbohydrate 102.5 g; Dietary Fibre 18.5 g; Cholesterol 0 mg; 2935 kJ (700 Cal)

RICH CHEESE MACARONI

Preparation time: 15 minutes
Cooking time: 40 minutes
Serves 4

450 g elbow macaroni
40 g butter
300 ml cream
125 g fontina cheese, sliced
125 g provolone cheese, grated
100 g Gruyère cheese, grated
125 g blue castello cheese, crumbled
1/2 cup (40 g) fresh white breadcrumbs
1/4 cup (25 g) grated Parmesan

1 Preheat the oven to moderate 180°C (350°F/Gas 4). Cook the pasta in a large saucepan of boiling water until *al dente*. Drain and keep warm. Melt half the butter in a large saucepan. Add the cream and, when just coming to the boil, add the fontina, provolone, Gruyère and blue castello cheeses, stirring constantly over low heat for 3 minutes, or until melted. Season with salt and ground white pepper. Add the pasta to the cheese mixture and mix well.

2 Spoon the mixture into a lightly greased shallow 2 litre ovenproof dish. Sprinkle with the breadcrumbs mixed with the Parmesan, dot with the remaining cubed butter and bake for 25 minutes, or until the top is golden and crisp. Serve with a salad.

NUTRITION PER SERVE
Fat 81 g; Protein 48.5 g; Carbohydrate 88.5 g; Dietary Fibre 6 g; Cholesterol 260 mg; 5330 kJ (1275 Cal)

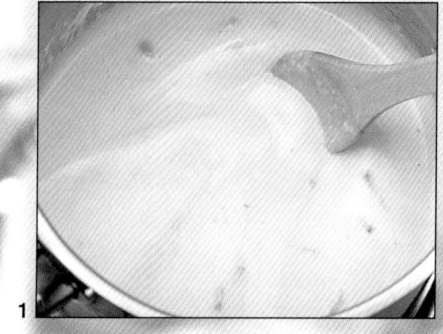

FRICELLI WITH MUSHROOMS AND ROCKET

Preparation time: 15 minutes +
    10 minutes soaking
Cooking time: 15 minutes
Serves 4

10 g dried porcini mushrooms
375 g fricelli
25 g butter
1/4 cup (60 ml) extra virgin olive oil
2 cloves garlic, crushed
250 g button mushrooms, sliced

1/4 cup (60 ml) lemon juice
1/3 cup (35 g) grated Parmesan
80 g baby rocket leaves, trimmed

1 Soak the porcini mushrooms in
1/3 cup (80 ml) boiling water for
10 minutes, or until softened. Cook
the pasta in a large saucepan of
boiling water until *al dente*. Drain
and return to the pan.
2 Meanwhile, heat the butter and
oil over medium heat in a frying
pan. Add the garlic and button
mushrooms and cook for 4 minutes,
tossing occasionally. Drain the
porcini mushrooms, reserving the

soaking liquid. Chop all of the
mushrooms, then add them to the
frying pan along with the reserved
soaking liquid. Bring to a simmer.
3 Add the mushroom mixture,
lemon juice and Parmesan to the
saucepan with the pasta and toss
together. Season to taste with salt
and cracked black pepper. Toss
through the rocket just before
serving. Spoon into warm serving
bowls and serve.

NUTRITION PER SERVE
Fat 22.5 g; Protein 16 g; Carbohydrate 68 g;
Dietary Fibre 7 g; Cholesterol 22 mg;
2265 kJ (540 Cal)

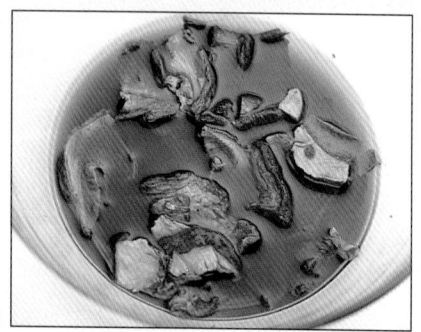

COTELLI WITH CAPERS, BOCCONCINI AND BASIL OIL

Preparation time: 10 minutes
Cooking time: 15 minutes
Serves 4–6

½ cup (125 ml) olive oil
125 g jar capers in brine, drained
500 g cotelli
2 tablespoons lemon juice
2 cups (100 g) firmly packed fresh basil
⅓ cup (35 g) grated Parmesan

250 g cherry tomatoes, quartered
8 bocconcini, quartered
extra virgin olive oil, for drizzling

1 Heat half the olive oil in a small saucepan, add the capers and cook over high heat for 3–4 minutes, or until crisp and golden. Drain on paper towels and set aside.

2 Cook the pasta in a large saucepan of boiling water until *al dente*. Drain and keep warm. Meanwhile, place the lemon juice, 1½ cups (75 g) of the basil and the remaining olive oil in a food processor and process until smooth. Season with salt and pepper.

3 Roughly tear the remaining basil leaves, then toss through the warm pasta with the basil mixture, 2 tablespoons of the Parmesan and the cherry tomatoes. Spoon into warmed bowls and top with the bocconcini and capers. Drizzle with extra virgin olive oil and garnish with the remaining grated Parmesan. Serve immediately.

NUTRITION PER SERVE (6)
Fat 26 g; Protein 21 g; Carbohydrate 61 g; Dietary Fibre 5.5 g; Cholesterol 23.5 mg; 2375 kJ (565 Cal)

SPEEDY GOULASH WITH FUSILLI

Preparation time: 15 minutes
Cooking time: 20 minutes
Serves 4

400 g fusilli
2 tablespoons olive oil
1 large onion, sliced into thin wedges
600 g rump steak, trimmed and cut into 2 cm cubes
1 tablespoon plain flour
1 small green capsicum, diced
2 x 425 g cans diced tomatoes (see Note)
1 teaspoon hot paprika
1/3 cup (80 g) light sour cream

1 Cook the pasta in a large saucepan of boiling water until *al dente*. Meanwhile, heat 1 tablespoon of the olive oil in a large frying pan, add the onion and cook, stirring, over medium heat for 4–5 minutes, or until softened and golden. Remove the onion from the pan.

2 Heat the remaining olive oil in the same pan. Toss the steak cubes in the flour, shaking off any excess, then add to the hot pan and cook for 2 minutes over high heat to brown on all sides. Add the capsicum, tomato, paprika and the cooked onion and stir to combine.

3 Bring the mixture to the boil, then reduce the heat and simmer for 8–10 minutes, stirring occasionally.

Season with salt and cracked black pepper. To serve, place the fusilli in serving bowls, spoon on the goulash mixture and top each serving with a tablespoon of sour cream.

NUTRITION PER SERVE
Fat 18.5 g; Protein 49.5 g; Carbohydrate 81.5 g; Dietary Fibre 8 g; Cholesterol 113 mg; 2925 kJ (700 Cal)

COOK'S FILE
Note: We used cans of tomatoes that are spiced with garlic and black pepper—they really added depth to the flavour of our goulash.

1

2

3

CRESTI DI GALLO WITH CREAMY TOMATO AND BACON SAUCE

Preparation time: 10 minutes
Cooking time: 15 minutes
Serves 4

400 g cresti di gallo
1 tablespoon olive oil
170 g streaky bacon, thinly sliced
(see Note)
500 g Roma tomatoes, roughly
chopped
1/2 cup (125 ml) thick cream
2 tablespoons sun-dried tomato
pesto
2 tablespoons finely chopped fresh
flat-leaf parsley
1/2 cup (50 g) finely grated Parmesan

1 Cook the pasta in a large saucepan of boiling water until *al dente*. Drain and return to the saucepan. Meanwhile, heat the oil in a frying pan, add the bacon and cook over high heat for 2 minutes, or until starting to brown. Reduce the heat to medium, add the tomato and cook, stirring frequently, for 2 minutes, or until the tomato has softened but still holds its shape.

2 Add the cream and tomato pesto and stir until heated through. Remove from the heat, add the parsley, then toss the sauce through the pasta with the grated Parmesan.

NUTRITION PER SERVE
Fat 28.5 g; Protein 24.5 g; Carbohydrate 75 g; Dietary Fibre 7 g; Cholesterol 62.5 mg; 2745 kJ (655 Cal)

COOK'S FILE
Note: Streaky bacon is the tail fatty ends of bacon rashers. It is fattier but adds to the flavour of the meal. You can use 170 g bacon rashers if you prefer.

WARM SWEET POTATO, ROCKET AND WALNUT SALAD

Preparation time: 15 minutes
Cooking time: 30 minutes
Serves 4

800 g orange sweet potato, cut into
   2 cm cubes
150 ml olive oil
1 cup (125 g) walnut pieces
350 g fricelli
150 g white castello cheese, softened
2 cloves garlic, crushed
2 teaspoons lemon juice
1/2 teaspoon sugar
100 g baby rocket or spinach leaves

1 Preheat the oven to moderately hot 200°C (400°F/Gas 6). Toss the orange sweet potato in 2 tablespoons of the oil and place in a single layer on a baking tray lined with baking paper. Season with salt and pepper. Cook, turning halfway through, for 30 minutes, or until golden and cooked through. Spread the walnuts onto a separate baking tray and add to the oven for the last 10 minutes, or until crisp and golden.

2 Meanwhile, cook the pasta in a large saucepan of boiling water until *al dente*. Drain, then return to the pan. Remove the rind from one third of the cheese and cut the rest into cubes. Finely chop 2 tablespoons of the toasted walnuts and place in a jar with the garlic, lemon juice, sugar, remaining oil and rindless cheese and season. Shake the jar until well combined. You may need to break the cheese up with a fork to help mix it through if it is too firm.

3 Toss the pasta, sweet potato, rocket, cubed cheese and remaining walnuts in a bowl, drizzle with the dressing and toss together. Divide among four serving bowls and season to taste with salt and black pepper.

NUTRITION PER SERVE
Fat 69 g; Protein 26.5 g; Carbohydrate 91.5 g;
Dietary Fibre 11 g; Cholesterol 37.5 mg;
4570 kJ (1090 Cal)

1

2

3

CHICKEN, BROCCOLI AND PASTA BAKE

Preparation time: 15 minutes
Cooking time: 35 minutes
Serves 6–8

300 g fusilli
425 g can cream of mushroom soup
2 eggs
3/4 cup (185 g) whole-egg mayonnaise
1 tablespoon Dijon mustard
1 2/3 cups (210 g) grated Cheddar
600 g chicken breast fillets, thinly
   sliced
400 g frozen broccoli pieces,
   thawed
1/2 cup (40 g) fresh breadcrumbs

1 Preheat the oven to moderate 180°C (350°/Gas 4). Cook the pasta in a large saucepan of boiling water until *al dente*, then drain and return to the pan. Combine the soup, eggs, mayonnaise, mustard and half the cheese in a bowl.

2 Heat a lightly greased non-stick frying pan over medium heat, add the chicken pieces and cook for 5–6 minutes, or until cooked through. Season with salt and pepper, then set aside to cool.

3 Add the chicken and broccoli to the pasta, pour the soup mixture over the top and stir until well combined. Transfer the mixture to a 3 litre ovenproof dish. Sprinkle with the combined breadcrumbs and remaining cheese. Bake for 20 minutes, or until the top becomes golden brown.

NUTRITION PER SERVE (8)
Fat 32.5 g; Protein 33.5 g; Carbohydrate 33 g; Dietary Fibre 4.5 g; Cholesterol 143 mg; 2340 kJ (560 Cal)

1

2

3

WARM LAMB, PASTA AND CHARGRILLED CAPSICUM SALAD

Preparation time: 15 minutes +
    10 minutes standing
Cooking time: 30 minutes
Serves 6

1/2 cup (125 ml) olive oil
1 tablespoon chopped fresh
    rosemary
2 cloves garlic, crushed
400 g lamb fillets (backstrap)
1/4 cup (60 g) wholegrain mustard
400 g fricelli
250 g snow peas, trimmed
2 cups (320 g) ready-made
    chargrilled, skinned red capsicum,
    thinly sliced (see Note)
100 g Swiss cheese, shaved

1 Preheat the oven to moderately hot 190°C (375°F/Gas 5). Place the oil, rosemary and garlic in a frying pan and cook, stirring, over low heat for 2 minutes, or until fragrant and lightly golden. Strain the oil into a large bowl, then return half of it to the pan. Add the rosemary and garlic to the bowl. Reheat the frying pan over high heat, add the lamb and cook for 30 seconds each side, or until browned. Transfer the lamb to a baking dish and roast for 8 minutes, then rest for 10 minutes.
2 Pour any remaining oil from the frying pan and any juices from the baking dish into the bowl with the rosemary and garlic. Add the mustard and stir together well. While the meat rests, cook the pasta in a large saucepan of boiling water until *al dente*. Drain and transfer to the bowl with the oil mixture. Bring a saucepan of water to the boil, add the snow peas and cook for 30 seconds, then drain and set aside.
3 Thinly slice the lamb on the diagonal and place in the bowl with the pasta. Add the snow peas, capsicum and two thirds of the cheese. Season with salt and pepper. Toss together well. Divide among four serving plates or bowls and sprinkle with the remaining cheese.

NUTRITION PER SERVE
Fat 21 g; Protein 29.5 g; Carbohydrate 51.5 g; Dietary Fibre 5.5 g; Cholesterol 59.5 mg; 2150 kJ (515 Cal)

COOK'S FILE
Note: You can buy chargrilled capsicum from the deli section of some of the big supermarkets. Alternatively, use a well-drained jar of chargrilled capsicum.

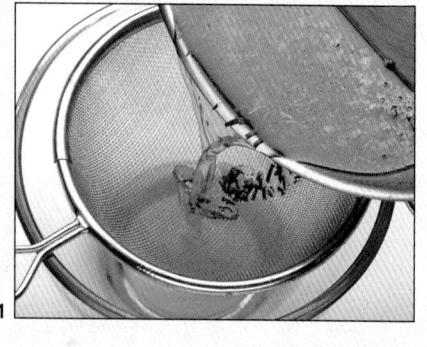

CRAB, CAMEMBERT AND FUSILLI FRITTATA

Preparation time: 15 minutes
Cooking time: 50 minutes
Serves 4–6

1 cup (80 g) tri-coloured fusilli
1 tablespoon olive oil
1 very small red onion, finely chopped
1 large Roma tomato, roughly chopped
1/3 cup (60 g) semi-dried tomatoes, roughly chopped
2 tablespoons finely chopped fresh coriander leaves
2/3 cup (140 g) cooked fresh or canned crab meat
150 g Camembert, rind removed, cut into small pieces
6 eggs plus 2 egg yolks

1 Cook the pasta in a large saucepan of boiling water until *al dente*. Drain, rinse, then drain again and set aside to cool. Meanwhile, heat half the oil in a small frying pan over low heat, add the onion and cook for 4–5 minutes, or until softened but not browned. Transfer to a bowl and add the Roma tomato, semi-dried tomatoes and coriander. Squeeze out any excess moisture from the crab meat and add the meat to the bowl. Add half the cheese to the bowl, then add the cooled pasta. Mix well. Beat together the six eggs and the two extra yolks, then stir into the tomato and crab mixture. Season.

2 Heat the remaining oil in the frying pan, pour in the frittata mixture and cook over low heat for 25 minutes. Preheat the grill to low. Scatter the remaining Camembert over the frittata before placing it under the grill for 10–15 minutes, or until cooked and golden brown on top. Remove from the grill and leave for 5 minutes. Cut into slices and serve with salad and some bread.

NUTRITION PER SERVE (6)
Fat 17 g; Protein 18.5 g; Carbohydrate 12.5 g; Dietary Fibre 2 g; Cholesterol 293 mg; 1155 kJ (275 Cal)

1

2

PEPPERED PORK, ZUCCHINI AND GARGANELLI

Preparation time: 15 minutes
Cooking time: 25 minutes
Serves 4

450 g pork fillet
3–4 teaspoons cracked black
   peppercorns
80 g butter
250 g garganelli
1 onion, halved and thinly sliced
2 large zucchini, thinly sliced
2/3 cup (20 g) fresh basil, torn
3/4 cup (155 g) baby black olives
1/2 cup (60 g) grated Romano cheese

1 Cut the pork fillet in half widthways and roll in the pepper and some salt. Heat half the butter in a large deep frying pan, add the pork and cook for 4 minutes each side, or until golden brown and just cooked through. Remove from the pan and cut into 5 mm slices, then set aside and keep warm.

2 Cook the pasta in a large saucepan of boiling water until *al dente*; drain well and return to the pan. Meanwhile, melt the remaining butter in the frying pan, add the onion and cook, stirring, over medium heat for about 3 minutes, or until soft. Add the zucchini and toss for 5 minutes, or until starting to soften. Add the basil, olives, sliced pork and any juices and toss well. Stir the pork mixture through the hot pasta, then season to taste with salt and cracked black pepper. Serve immediately topped with the cheese.

NUTRITION PER SERVE
Fat 21.5 g; Protein 38.5 g; Carbohydrate 52.5 g; Dietary Fibre 5 g; Cholesterol 113.5 mg; 2340 kJ (560 Cal)

CREAMY PORK AND APPLE WITH FRICELLI

Preparation time: 15 minutes
Cooking time: 25 minutes
Serves 4

375 g fricelli
60 g butter
2 Granny Smith apples, peeled, cored and cut into thin wedges
2 pork fillets (500 g in total), thinly sliced
1½ cups (375 ml) chicken stock
1 cup (250 ml) dry alcoholic cider
3 teaspoons wholegrain mustard
2 cloves garlic, crushed
2/3 cup (170 ml) thick cream

1 Cook the pasta in a large saucepan of boiling water until *al dente*. Drain, cover and set aside to keep warm. Meanwhile, heat 20 g of the butter in a large frying pan, add the apple and cook over high heat, turning occasionally, for 4 minutes until golden. Remove from the pan, cover and keep warm. Add 20 g butter to the same pan and stir-fry half the pork for 2–3 minutes, or until seared and just browned, remove from the pan and keep warm. Repeat with the remaining butter and pork.
2 Add the stock, cider, mustard and garlic to the pan and boil for about 10 minutes, or until the sauce has reduced by half, scraping up any sediment with a wooden spoon. Reduce the heat to medium and add the cream, pork and any cooking juices and cook for 2–3 minutes, or until the pork is just cooked through and tender.
3 Stir in two thirds of the apple, being careful not to break it up, then mix in the pasta. Serve topped with a few pieces of the remaining apple.

NUTRITION PER SERVE
Fat 30 g; Protein 40 g; Carbohydrate 78.5 g; Dietary Fibre 6.5 g; Cholesterol 199 mg; 3195 kJ (765 Cal)

COOK'S FILE
Note: Don't use a non-stick frying pan to cook the apples because they will not caramelise properly.

WARM MINTED CHICKEN AND PASTA SALAD

Preparation time: 15 minutes
Cooking time: 20 minutes
Serves 4

250 g cotelli
1/2 cup (125 ml) olive oil
1 large red capsicum
3 chicken breast fillets
6 spring onions, cut into 2 cm lengths
4 cloves garlic, thinly sliced
3/4 cup (35 g) chopped fresh mint
1/3 cup (80 ml) cider vinegar
100 g baby spinach leaves

1 Cook the pasta in a large saucepan of boiling water until *al dente*, drain, stir in 1 tablespoon of the oil and set aside. Meanwhile, cut the capsicum into quarters, removing the seeds and membrane. Place, skin-side-up, under a hot grill for 8–10 minutes, or until the skin blackens and blisters. Cool in a plastic bag, then peel away the skin. Cut into thin strips. Place the chicken between two sheets of plastic wrap and press with the palm of your hand until slightly flattened.
2 Heat 1 tablespoon of the oil in a large frying pan, add the chicken and cook over medium heat for 2–3 minutes each side, or until light brown and cooked through. Remove from the pan and cut into 5 mm slices.
3 Add another tablespoon of the oil to the pan and add the spring onion, garlic and capsicum and cook, stirring, for 2–3 minutes, or until starting to soften. Add 1/2 cup (25 g) of the mint, the vinegar and the remaining oil and stir until warmed through. In a large bowl, combine the pasta, chicken, spinach, onion mixture and remaining mint and toss well, seasoning to taste. Serve warm.

NUTRITION PER SERVE
Fat 30 g; Protein 47 g; Carbohydrate 46.5 g; Dietary Fibre 5.5 g; Cholesterol 84 mg; 2705 kJ (645 Cal)

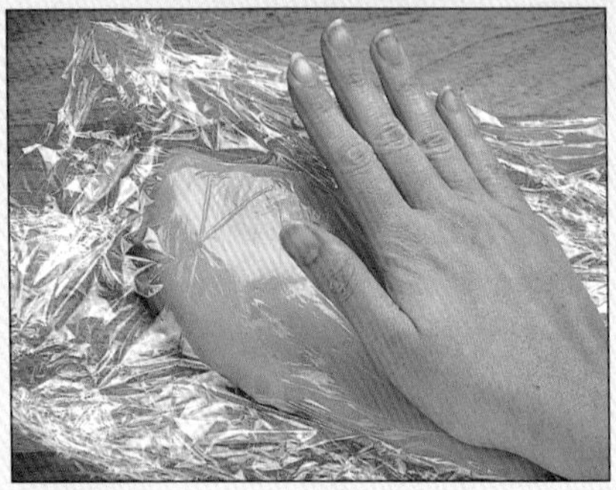

COTELLI, TOMATO AND ARTICHOKE GRILL

Preparation time: 15 minutes
Cooking time: 20 minutes
Serves 4

350 g cotelli
285 g jar marinated artichoke hearts, drained and chopped
2 tablespoons olive oil
1 cup (250 ml) thick cream
2 tablespoons chopped fresh thyme
2 cloves garlic, crushed
3/4 cup (75 g) grated Parmesan
1 2/3 cups (210 g) grated Cheddar
950 g tomatoes, sliced into 0.5 cm slices

1 Cook the pasta in a large saucepan of boiling water until *al dente*. Drain and return to the pan. Grease a 23 cm x 30 cm rectangular ovenproof dish. Stir the artichokes, olive oil, cream, thyme, garlic, half the Parmesan and 1 1/4 cups (155 g) of the Cheddar through the hot pasta and season well. Spread evenly into the prepared dish.

2 Arrange the tomatoes over the top, overlapping one another. Season, then sprinkle the remaining Cheddar and Parmesan over the top. Cook under a hot grill for 6 minutes, or until the cheeses melt and turn a golden brown.

NUTRITION PER SERVE
Fat 55.5 g; Protein 33 g; Carbohydrate 69 g; Dietary Fibre 9 g; Cholesterol 137 mg; 3800 kJ (910 Cal)

ANGEL HAIR PASTA

BUCATINI

FETTUCINE

LINGUINE

SPAGHETTI

SPAGHETTINI

TAGLIATELLE

VERMICELLI

ZITI

LONG

Fresh or dried, long pasta may not be the tidiest of meals, but the sensation of eating the thin strands makes it all worthwhile.

ANGEL HAIR PASTA: Also called capelli d'angelo, this pasta is only available in dried form and it is the thinnest of all the spaghetti pastas. Resembling strands of long, blonde hair, its fine texture is best suited for use in broths and with extremely delicate, light, smooth sauces. Angel hair pasta can be replaced with capellini (not shown), spaghettini or vermicelli.

BUCATINI: Similar to thick spaghetti but with a hollow centre that helps it cook more quickly than spaghetti. Bucatini means small hole in Italian. It is traditionally served with carbonara and Amatriciana sauces. You can substitute linguine, spaghetti or one of the longer fusilli pastas (page 31) for bucatini.

FETTUCINE: This pasta is slightly narrower and thicker than the very similar pasta, tagliatelle. It is usually served with rich, creamy sauces or simple fresh flavours, because the thickness of the strands helps it to carry the accompanying sauce. You can use trenette (not shown) or tagliatelle instead. There are several varieties of this very popular pasta; we have used only a few of the many types available.
Fresh spinach fettucine: Also known as *fettucine verde* due to its rich green colour, it is made by the addition of cooked, well-drained spinach to the dough before it is kneaded. The most popular of the coloured pastas, its colour makes it an attractive companion to both red tomato-based sauces and white cream-based ones.
Fresh basil fettucine: While it is uncommon to find herbs in pasta as they are usually included in the sauce, there are some regional specialities which incorporate finely chopped herbs, such as basil, in the pasta dough. When using a herb-flavoured pasta, choose simple sauces whose flavours won't compete with or overshadow the flavour of the pasta. These speciality pastas are usually only available home-made or in pasta shops.

LINGUINE (fresh, dried): The Italian word for 'little tongues', linguine is a long flat pasta also known as bavette. It is good with pesto or seafood sauces. Substitute bucatini, fettucine, spaghetti, tagliatelle or long fusilli (page 31), remembering that if the recipe asks for fresh pasta, use fresh and if it asks for dried, use dried.

SPAGHETTI (fresh, dried): The name of this very popular pasta comes from the Italian word 'strings'. Nowadays, spaghetti is made all over the world. The commercial making of spaghetti involves pushing the pasta dough through an extrusion system to make the noodles. Out of all the hundreds of pasta shapes, spaghetti is the most versatile. It is suitable for a large number of sauces and it comes in 2–3 different thicknesses, one being thin spaghetti, also known as spaghettini. Substitute bucatini or spaghettini. Always replace fresh pasta with fresh and dried pasta with dried.

SPAGHETTINI: Very similar to spaghetti, but even thinner, these so-called 'little lengths of cord' make an ideal match for delicate, oil-based sauces such as the Italian classic aglio e olio (garlic and olive oil) or fish and shellfish sauces. Spaghettini is often only available as dried pasta. Substitute other long, fine pastas such as angel hair pasta, spaghetti or vermicelli.

TAGLIATELLE (fresh, dried): Slightly wider than fettucine, these very thin, flat ribbon noodles are the northern Italian name for fettucine. In fact, the two are interchangeable. Tagliatelle, *not* spaghetti, is the traditional accompaniment to Bolognese sauce. Unlike other pasta shapes, both fresh and dried tagliatelle are made with the addition of egg to the pasta dough. Like other ribbon pastas, it is at its best when accompanied by light cream or butter-based sauces, or fresh flavours. You can substitute lasagnette (page 91) or fettucine.

VERMICELLI: Meaning 'little worms' in Italian, it is a very fine, long pasta best eaten in broth-based noodle soups or with fine-textured tomato, butter or cheese sauces which cling well to its length. Vermicelli is thinner than spaghetti. Replace with spaghettini or angel hair pasta.

ZITI: A long, tubular pasta, its strong, thick texture and hollow interior are excellent for picking up heavy meat sauces such as ragus and chunky vegetable sauces. Unlike other long pastas, it is often broken into smaller pieces prior to cooking. It can be replaced with pasta of a similar size like candele (not shown), lasagnette (page 91), rigatoni, penne (page 7) or bucatini.

SPAGHETTI BOLOGNESE

Preparation time: 10 minutes
Cooking time: 55 minutes
Serves 4

1 tablespoon olive oil
1 large onion, diced
2 cloves garlic, crushed
600 g beef mince (you can also
    use veal and beef mince)
1/2 cup (125 ml) red wine
1/2 cup (125 ml) beef stock
2 x 400 g cans chopped tomatoes
1 carrot, grated
350 g spaghetti

1 Heat the oil over medium heat in a large saucepan, add the onion and garlic and cook for 1–2 minutes, or until soft. Add the mince and cook, stirring to break up any lumps, for 5 minutes, or until the meat is browned. Pour in the wine and simmer for 2–3 minutes, or until reduced slightly, then add the stock and simmer for a further 2 minutes. Add the tomato and carrot and season well with salt and pepper. Cook over low heat for 40 minutes.
2 About 15 minutes before serving time, cook the pasta in a large saucepan of boiling water until *al dente*. Drain well and keep warm. Divide the pasta evenly among four serving bowls and pour the meat sauce over the pasta. Garnish with parsley, if desired.

NUTRITION PER SERVE
Fat 22.5 g; Protein 42.5 g; Carbohydrate 70.5 g; Dietary Fibre 8 g; Cholesterol 94.5 mg; 2830 kJ (675 Cal)

COOK'S FILE
Hint: Delicious with grated Parmesan.

1

2

BUCATINI WITH SAUSAGE AND FENNEL SEED

Preparation time: 10 minutes
Cooking time: 40 minutes
Serves 4

500 g good-quality Italian sausages
2 tablespoons olive oil
3 cloves garlic, chopped
1 teaspoon fennel seeds
1/2 teaspoon chilli flakes
2 x 425 g cans crushed tomatoes
500 g bucatini
1 teaspoon balsamic vinegar
1/4 cup (7 g) loosely packed fresh
   basil, chopped

1 Heat a frying pan over high heat, add the sausages and cook, turning, for 8–10 minutes, or until well browned and cooked through. Remove, cool slightly and slice on the diagonal into 1 cm pieces.

2 Heat the oil in a saucepan, add the garlic and cook over medium heat for 1 minute. Add the fennel seeds and chilli flakes and cook for a further minute. Stir in the tomato and bring to the boil, then reduce the heat and simmer, covered, for 20 minutes. Meanwhile, cook the pasta in a large saucepan of boiling water until *al dente*. Drain and return to the pan to keep warm.

3 Add the sausages to the sauce and cook, uncovered, for 5 minutes to heat through. Stir in the balsamic vinegar and basil. Divide the pasta among four bowls, top with the sauce and serve.

NUTRITION PER SERVE
Fat 50.5 g; Protein 34 g; Carbohydrate 96 g; Dietary Fibre 9.5 g; Cholesterol 95 mg; 4125 kJ (985 Cal)

LINGUINE WITH HAM, ARTICHOKE AND LEMON SAUCE

Preparation time: 15 minutes
Cooking time: 10 minutes
Serves 4

500 g fresh linguine
25 g butter
2 large cloves garlic, chopped
150 g marinated artichokes, drained
    and quartered
150 g sliced leg ham, cut into strips
300 ml cream
2 teaspoons coarsely grated lemon
    rind
1/2 cup (15 g) fresh basil, torn
1/3 cup (35 g) grated Parmesan

1 Cook the pasta in a large saucepan of boiling water until *al dente*. Drain, then return to the pan. Meanwhile, melt the butter in a large frying pan, add the garlic and cook over medium heat for 1 minute, or until fragrant. Add the artichokes and ham and cook for a further 2 minutes.

2 Add the cream and lemon rind, reduce the heat and simmer for 5 minutes, gently breaking up the artichokes with a wooden spoon. Pour the sauce over the pasta, then add the basil and Parmesan and toss well until the pasta is evenly coated. Divide among four serving plates and serve immediately.

NUTRITION PER SERVE
Fat 42 g; Protein 25.5 g; Carbohydrate 90.5 g; Dietary Fibre 7.5 g; Cholesterol 143 mg; 3540 kJ (845 Cal)

FRESH FETTUCINE WITH BALSAMIC SEARED TUNA CHUNKS

Preparation time: 15 minutes +
  10 minutes marinating
Cooking time: 15 minutes
Serves 4–6

4 x 200 g tuna steaks
2/3 cup (170 ml) balsamic vinegar
1/2 cup (125 ml) good-quality olive oil
1 lemon
1 clove garlic, finely chopped
1 red onion, finely chopped
2 tablespoons capers, rinsed and dried
1/2 cup (10 g) fresh flat-leaf parsley,
  finely chopped
500 g fresh fettucine

1 Place the tuna in a non-metallic dish and cover with the balsamic vinegar. Turn to coat evenly with the vinegar and marinate for 10 minutes. Heat 2 tablespoons of the oil in a large frying pan over medium heat and cook the tuna steaks for 2–3 minutes each side. Remove from the pan, cut into 2 cm cubes and transfer to a bowl.

2 Finely grate the rind from the lemon to give 1/2 teaspoon rind, then squeeze the lemon to give 1/4 cup (60 ml) juice. Wipe the frying pan clean, and heat 2 tablespoons of the olive oil over medium heat, then add the garlic and cook for 30 seconds. Stir in the chopped onion and cook for 2 minutes. Add the lemon rind and capers and cook for 1 minute, then stir in the parsley and cook for 1 minute. Add the lemon juice and remaining oil and gently toss together. Season to taste.

3 Meanwhile, cook the pasta in a large saucepan of boiling water until *al dente*. Drain well, return to the pan and toss the caper mixture through. Divide the pasta among serving bowls and arrange the tuna pieces over the top.

NUTRITION PER SERVE (6)
Fat 26 g; Protein 43 g; Carbohydrate 60 g; Dietary Fibre 4.5 g; Cholesterol 48 mg; 2740 kJ (655 Cal)

1

2

3

TAGLIATELLE WITH SALMON ROE AND HERB BREADCRUMBS

Preparation time: 15 minutes
Cooking time: 20 minutes
Serves 6

8 slices white bread
250 g mascarpone
2 egg yolks
4 cloves garlic, peeled
200 ml olive oil
500 g fresh tagliatelle
3 tablespoons chopped fresh dill
100 g Parmesan, grated
60 g salmon roe

1 Place the slices of bread in a food processor or blender and process until fine breadcrumbs form. Remove from the food processor. Place the mascarpone, egg yolks and 1 clove chopped garlic in the food processor or blender and process until smooth. With the motor running, gradually add half the oil in a thin stream.
2 Cook the pasta in a large saucepan of boiling water until *al dente*, then drain. Meanwhile, heat the remaining oil in a heavy-based frying pan and cook the remaining garlic cloves over medium heat for 2–3 minutes, or until golden brown. Remove the cloves from the oil and discard. Add the fresh breadcrumbs to the warm

oil and cook over low heat for 15 minutes, or until golden and crunchy. Remove from the pan and drain on paper towels. When cool, stir in the dill and season lightly with salt and cracked black pepper.
3 Add the mascarpone mixture and the Parmesan to the pasta and toss together well. Divide among six serving plates, sprinkle with the breadcrumbs, top with the salmon roe and serve immediately.

NUTRITION PER SERVE
Fat 54 g; Protein 25.5 g; Carbohydrate 77.5 g; Dietary Fibre 5.5 g; Cholesterol 151.5 mg; 3745 kJ (895 Cal)

1

2

3

SPAGHETTI WITH HERB, GARLIC AND CHILLI OIL

Preparation time: 15 minutes
Cooking time: 15 minutes
Serves 4–6

1 cup (250 ml) good-quality olive oil
2 bird's eye chillies, seeded and thinly
    sliced
5–6 large cloves garlic, crushed
500 g spaghetti
100 g thinly sliced prosciutto
1/2 cup (30 g) chopped fresh flat-leaf
    parsley
2 tablespoons chopped fresh basil
2 tablespoons chopped fresh
    oregano
3/4 cup (75 g) good-quality grated
    Parmesan

1 Pour the oil into a small saucepan with the chilli and garlic. Slowly heat the oil over low heat for about 12 minutes to infuse the oil with the garlic and chilli. Don't allow the oil to reach smoking point or the garlic will burn and taste bitter.
2 Meanwhile, cook the pasta in a large saucepan of boiling water until *al dente*. Drain well and return to the pan. Lay the prosciutto on a grill tray and grill under a hot grill for 2 minutes each side, or until crispy. Cool and break into pieces.
3 Pour the hot oil mixture over the spaghetti and toss well with the prosciutto, fresh herbs and Parmesan. Season to taste.

NUTRITION PER SERVE (6)
Fat 44 g; Protein 17.5 g; Carbohydrate 59.5 g; Dietary Fibre 5.5 g; Cholesterol 20.5 mg; 2945 kJ (705 Cal)

COOK'S FILE
Note: This is a very simple dish, but it relies on good-quality ingredients.

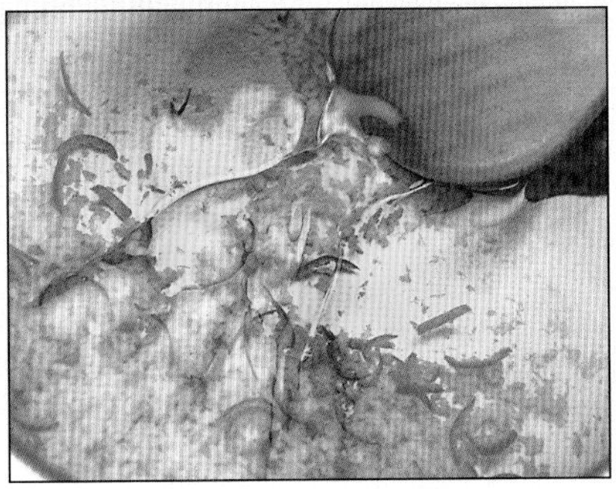

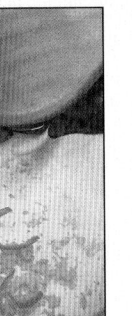
1

2

3

LINGUINE WITH BROCCOLI, PINE NUTS AND LEMON

Preparation time: 15 minutes
Cooking time: 15 minutes
Serves 4–6

500 g linguine
600 g broccoli, cut into small florets
1/2 cup (80 g) pine nuts
1/2 cup (125 ml) extra virgin olive oil
2 teaspoons finely grated lemon rind
1/4 cup (60 ml) lemon juice
1 teaspoon dried chilli flakes
1/2 cup (50 g) finely grated good-quality Parmesan

1 Cook the pasta in a large saucepan of boiling water until *al dente*. Drain and return to the pan. Meanwhile, bring a saucepan of water to the boil and cook the broccoli for 2 minutes, or until just tender but still bright green. Drain and set aside.

2 Heat a large non-stick frying pan and toast the pine nuts for 2–3 minutes, or until just golden, shaking the pan to prevent them burning. Remove from the pan and roughly chop. Reduce the heat to low, add the oil and lemon rind to the frying pan and gently heat until fragrant. Add the broccoli, chopped nuts, lemon juice and chilli and stir until warmed through. Season. Add to the pasta with the Parmesan and toss to combine. Divide among serving bowls and serve.

NUTRITION PER SERVE (6)
Fat 27 g; Protein 19 g; Carbohydrate 60 g; Dietary Fibre 9 g; Cholesterol 8 mg; 2355 kJ (560 Cal)

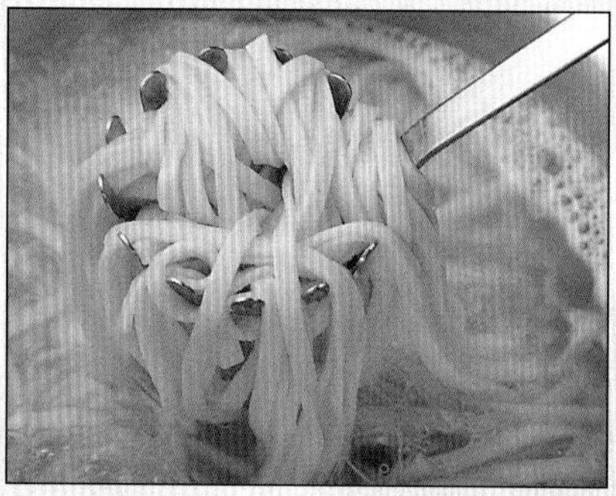

SPAGHETTI NICOISE

Preparation time: 10 minutes
Cooking time: 15 minutes
Serves 4–6

350 g spaghetti
8 quail eggs (or 4 hen eggs)
1 lemon
3 x 185 g cans good-quality tuna
   in oil
1/3 cup (50 g) pitted and halved
   Kalamata olives
100 g semi-dried tomatoes, halved
   lengthways

4 anchovy fillets chopped into small
   pieces
3 tablespoons baby capers, drained
3 tablespoons chopped fresh flat-leaf
   parsley

1 Cook the pasta in a large saucepan of boiling water until *al dente*. Meanwhile, place the eggs in a saucepan of cold water, bring to the boil and cook for 4 minutes (10 minutes for hen eggs). Drain, cool under cold water, then peel. Cut the quail eggs into halves or the hen eggs into quarters. Finely grate the rind of the lemon to give 1 teaspoon of grated rind. Then, squeeze the lemon to give 2 tablespoons juice.
2 Empty the tuna and its oil into a large bowl. Add the olives, tomato halves, anchovies, lemon rind and juice, capers and 2 tablespoons of the parsley. Drain the pasta and rinse in a little cold water, then toss gently through the tuna mixture. Divide among serving bowls, garnish with egg and the extra chopped fresh parsley, and serve.

NUTRITION PER SERVE (6)
Fat 26 g; Protein 31.5 g; Carbohydrate 46.5 g; Dietary Fibre 4.5 g; Cholesterol 152.5 mg; 2300 kJ (550 Cal)

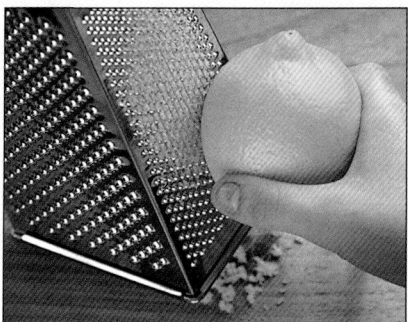

TAGLIATELLE WITH SALMON AND CREAMY DILL DRESSING

Preparation time: 10 minutes
Cooking time: 15 minutes
Serves 4

350 g fresh tagliatelle
1/4 cup (60 ml) olive oil
3 x 200 g salmon fillets, skinned and boned (ask your fishmonger to do this for you)
3 cloves garlic, crushed
1 1/2 cups (375 ml) cream
1 1/2 tablespoons chopped fresh dill
1 teaspoon mustard powder
1 tablespoon lemon juice
40 g shaved Parmesan

1 Cook the pasta in a large saucepan of boiling water until *al dente*. Drain, then toss with 1 tablespoon oil. Meanwhile, heat the remaining oil in a large deep frying pan and cook the salmon for 2 minutes each side, or until crisp on the outside but still pink inside. Remove from the pan, cut into 2 cm cubes, and keep warm.
2 In the same pan, add the garlic and cook for 30 seconds, or until fragrant. Add the cream, dill and mustard powder, bring to the boil, then reduce the heat and simmer, stirring, for 4–5 minutes, or until thickened. Season.
3 Add the salmon and any juices plus the lemon juice to the creamy dill sauce and stir until warmed through. Gently toss the sauce and salmon through the pasta and divide among four serving bowls. Sprinkle with the Parmesan and serve.

NUTRITION PER SERVE
Fat 66 g; Protein 45 g; Carbohydrate 51 g; Dietary Fibre 1.5 g; Cholesterol 215 mg; 4100 kJ (980 Cal)

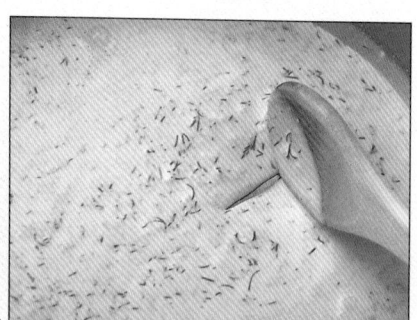

SPAGHETTI PRIMAVERA

Preparation time: 15 minutes
Cooking time: 15 minutes
Serves 4

400 g spaghetti
1/3 cup (80 ml) extra virgin olive oil
200 g fresh asparagus, trimmed
    and cut into 5 cm lengths
1 cup (155 g) frozen peas
1 cup (155 g) frozen broad beans
1 leek, thinly sliced
2 tablespoons finely chopped fresh
    flat-leaf parsley
1 cup (250 ml) thick cream
1/3 cup (35 g) grated Parmesan

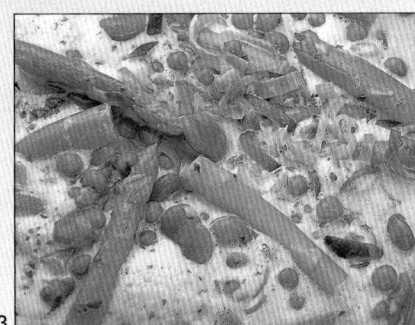

1 Cook the pasta in a large saucepan of boiling water until *al dente*. Rinse and drain well, then return to the pan, toss with 2 tablespoons of the oil and keep warm.

2 Meanwhile, bring a saucepan of water to the boil and cook the asparagus and peas for 2 minutes, or until bright green and tender. Remove with a slotted spoon and plunge into cold water. Return the saucepan to the boil and cook the broad beans for 2 minutes, or until tender. Drain, cool a little, then slip off their skins.

3 Heat the remaining oil in a frying pan and cook the leek over low heat for 2–3 minutes, or until soft but not brown. Add the blanched vegetables and cook for 1 minute, or until warmed through. Stir in the parsley and cream and simmer for 2–3 minutes. Toss the sauce and Parmesan through the pasta, season well with salt and cracked black pepper and serve.

NUTRITION PER SERVE
Fat 43 g; Protein 21 g; Carbohydrate 77 g; Dietary Fibre 10.5 g; Cholesterol 78 mg; 3270 kJ (780 Cal)

COOK'S FILE
Note: If fresh broad beans and peas are in season, use them and peel the pods before cooking.

TAGLIATELLE WITH FETA, TOMATO AND ROCKET

Preparation time: 15 minutes
Cooking time: 15 minutes
Serves 4

4 vine-ripened tomatoes
1 small red onion, finely chopped
4 tablespoons shredded fresh basil
2 tablespoons olive oil
375 g tagliatelle
2 cloves garlic, finely chopped
150 g baby rocket leaves
150 g soft feta, crumbled
1/4 cup (15 g) fresh small whole
    basil leaves

1 Score a cross in the base of each tomato, then place in a bowl of boiling water for 1 minute. Plunge into cold water and peel the skin away from the cross. Cut in half and remove the seeds with a teaspoon. Chop, then transfer to a bowl. Add the onion and basil, stir in 1 tablespoon of the oil and set aside.
2 Cook the pasta in a large saucepan of boiling water until *al dente*. Drain, reserving 1/2 cup (125 ml) pasta water. Return the pasta to the pan, add the remaining oil, the garlic and the reserved pasta water and toss together over medium heat for 1–2 minutes to warm through. Stir in the tomato mixture, rocket and feta. Season to taste with salt and pepper. Divide among four serving plates and serve immediately garnished with the whole basil leaves.

NUTRITION PER SERVE
Fat 18 g; Protein 20 g; Carbohydrate 70.5 g; Dietary Fibre 7.5 g; Cholesterol 26 mg; 2205 kJ (525 Cal)

1

2

ANGEL HAIR PASTA WITH SCALLOPS AND ROCKET

Preparation time: 15 minutes
Cooking time: 15 minutes
Serves 4

350 g angel hair pasta
100 g butter
3 cloves garlic, crushed
24 scallops, without roe
150 g baby rocket leaves
2 teaspoons finely grated lemon rind
1/4 cup (60 ml) lemon juice
125 g semi-dried tomatoes, thinly
    sliced
30 g shaved Parmesan

1 Cook the pasta in a large saucepan of boiling water until *al dente*. Meanwhile, melt the butter in a small saucepan, add the garlic and cook over low heat, stirring, for 1 minute. Remove from the heat.
2 Heat a lightly greased chargrill plate over high heat and cook the scallops, brushing occasionally with some of the garlic butter for 1–2 minutes each side, or until cooked. Set aside and keep warm.
3 Drain the pasta and return to the pan with the remaining garlic butter, the rocket, lemon rind, lemon juice and tomato and toss until combined. Divide among four serving plates and top with the scallops. Season to taste and sprinkle with Parmesan.

NUTRITION PER SERVE
Fat 25.5 g; Protein 25 g; Carbohydrate 69 g; Dietary Fibre 7.5 g; Cholesterol 97 mg; 2545 kJ (610 Cal)

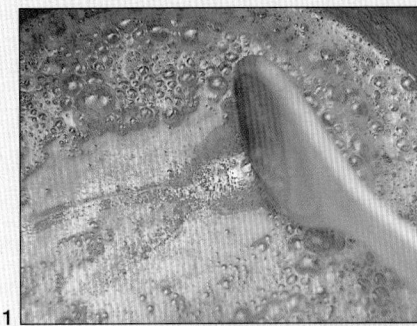

FETTUCINE WITH CREAMY SPINACH AND ROAST TOMATO

Preparation time: 10 minutes
Cooking time: 35 minutes
Serves 4–6

6 Roma tomatoes
40 g butter
2 cloves garlic, crushed
1 onion, chopped
500 g English spinach, trimmed
1 cup (250 ml) vegetable stock
½ cup (125 ml) thick cream
500 g fresh spinach fettucine
50 g shaved Parmesan

1 Preheat the oven to hot 220°C (425°F/Gas 7). Cut the tomatoes in half lengthways, then cut each half into three wedges. Place the wedges on a lightly greased baking tray and bake for 30–35 minutes, or until softened and slightly golden. Meanwhile, heat the butter in a large frying pan. Add the garlic and onion and cook over medium heat for 5 minutes, or until the onion is soft. Add the spinach, stock and cream, increase the heat to high and bring to the boil. Simmer rapidly for 5 minutes.

2 While the spinach mixture is cooking, cook the pasta in a large saucepan of boiling water until *al dente*. Drain and return to the pan. Remove the spinach from the heat and season well. Cool slightly, then process in a food processor until smooth. Toss through the pasta until well coated. Divide among serving bowls, top with the roasted tomatoes and Parmesan shavings.

NUTRITION PER SERVE (6)
Fat 17.5 g; Protein 17 g; Carbohydrate 65 g; Dietary Fibre 7.5 g; Cholesterol 49 mg; 2035 kJ (485 Cal)

SPAGHETTI WITH SMOKED TUNA AND OLIVES

Preparation time: 15 minutes
Cooking time: 20 minutes
Serves 4

800 g vine-ripened tomatoes
375 g spaghetti
3 x 125 g cans smoked tuna slices
    in oil
1 red onion, chopped
2 cloves garlic, crushed
1 teaspoon sugar
150 g black olives
2 tablespoons chopped fresh basil
75 g Greek feta, crumbled

1 Score a cross in the base of each tomato. Place the tomatoes in a bowl of boiling water for 1 minute, then plunge into cold water and peel the skin away from the cross. Cut in half and remove the seeds with a teaspoon. Roughly chop the flesh. Cook the pasta in a large saucepan of boiling water until *al dente*. Drain and keep warm.

2 Drain the oil from the tuna slices, reserving 1 tablespoon. Heat the reserved oil in a large saucepan, add the onion and cook over low heat for 3–4 minutes, or until soft but not brown. Add the garlic and cook for another minute, then add the chopped tomatoes and sugar. Cook over medium heat for 8–10 minutes, or until pulpy.

3 Add the tuna slices, olives and chopped basil, stir well and cook for 2 minutes, or until warmed through. Toss through the spaghetti and season with salt and cracked black pepper. Sprinkle with crumbled feta and serve immediately, accompanied by shaved Parmesan if desired.

NUTRITION PER SERVE
Fat 19 g; Protein 40 g; Carbohydrate 83 g; Dietary Fibre 7.5 g; Cholesterol 50.5 mg; 2795 kJ (670 Cal)

1

2

3

SPAGHETTI MARINARA

Preparation time: 15 minutes
Cooking time: 35 minutes
Serves 4–6

2 tablespoons olive oil
1 onion, finely chopped
2 cloves garlic, crushed
2 x 400 g cans diced tomatoes
1/4 cup (60 g) tomato paste
500 g spaghetti
500 g good-quality marinara mix
  (see Note)
8 black mussels, beards removed,
  scrubbed
2 tablespoons shredded fresh
  basil

1 Heat the oil in a saucepan over medium heat, add the onion and cook for 5 minutes, or until softened and lightly browned. Add the garlic and stir for another 1 minute, or until aromatic. Add the tomato and tomato paste and bring to the boil, then reduce the heat and simmer for 20–25 minutes, or until the sauce becomes rich and pulpy. Stir the sauce occasionally during cooking. Season with salt and cracked black pepper. Meanwhile, cook the pasta in a large saucepan of boiling water until *al dente*. Drain well, return to the saucepan and keep warm.
2 Add the marinara mix and the mussels to the tomato sauce and cook for about 2–3 minutes, or until the seafood is cooked and the mussels are open. Discard any mussels that do not open. Stir in the basil. Toss the sauce through the warm pasta and serve.

NUTRITION PER SERVE (6)
Fat 10 g; Protein 34 g; Carbohydrate 68.5 g; Dietary Fibre 6 g; Cholesterol 131 mg; 2125 kJ (510 Cal)

COOK'S FILE
Note: Marinara mix is available from your seafood store. Try to choose a good-quality marinara mix to avoid chewy seafood. Alternatively, you can make your own by choosing a few different types of seafood, such as octopus, fish fillets and calamari and chop into bite-size pieces.

ANGEL HAIR PASTA WITH CREAMY GARLIC PRAWNS

Preparation time: 15 minutes
Cooking time: 15 minutes
Serves 4

2 tablespoons olive oil
16 raw medium prawns, peeled
1 leek, chopped
6 cloves garlic, crushed
1/2 teaspoon dried chilli flakes
1/2 cup (125 ml) dry white wine
200 ml cream
250 g angel hair pasta
3 tablespoons chopped fresh
    flat-leaf parsley

1 Heat half the oil in a frying pan, season the prawns with salt and pepper, add to the pan and cook over high heat for 2–3 minutes, or until cooked through. Remove from the pan, cover and keep warm.

2 Heat the remaining oil in the same pan, add the leek and cook, stirring, over medium heat for 2–3 minutes, or until softened. Add the garlic and chilli flakes and stir for 1 minute. Pour in the wine, reduce the heat and simmer for 4 minutes, or until reduced. Add the cream and simmer for 3 minutes, or until just thickened.

3 Meanwhile, cook the pasta in a large saucepan of boiling water until *al dente*. Drain and return to the pan. Stir the parsley into the sauce and season well. Add to the pasta and stir to coat. Divide among the serving bowls and top with prawns.

NUTRITION PER SERVE
Fat 32 g; Protein 19.5 g; Carbohydrate 48.5 g; Dietary Fibre 4.5 g; Cholesterol 142.5 mg; 2420 kJ (580 Cal)

1

2

3

SPAGHETTI WITH SHELLFISH AND WHITE WINE SAUCE

Preparation time: 15 minutes
Cooking time: 10 minutes
Serves 4

500 g mussels
1 kg clams
400 g fresh spaghetti
2 tablespoons olive oil
4 French shallots, finely chopped
2 cloves garlic, crushed
1 cup (250 ml) dry white wine
3 tablespoons chopped fresh
    flat-leaf parsley

1 Scrub the mussels with a stiff brush and remove any barnacles with a knife. Remove the beards. Discard any mussels or clams that are broken or open ones that do not close when tapped on the work surface. Wash them both thoroughly under cold running water. Cook the pasta in a large saucepan of boiling water until *al dente*. Drain and keep warm in a large saucepan.

2 Meanwhile, heat the oil in a large saucepan over medium heat and cook the shallots for 4 minutes, or until softened. Add the garlic and cook for a further 1 minute. Pour in the wine, bring to the boil and cook for 2 minutes, or until reduced slightly. Add the clams and mussels, tossing to coat them in the liquid, then cover the pan. Cook, shaking the pan regularly, for about 3 minutes, or until the shells have opened. Discard any clams or mussels that do not open. Toss the clam mixture through the spaghetti, scatter with parsley and transfer to a warmed serving dish. Season and serve with salad and bread.

NUTRITION PER SERVE
Fat 12 g; Protein 36.5 g; Carbohydrate 75.5 g; Dietary Fibre 5.5 g; Cholesterol 67.5 mg; 2520 kJ (600 Cal)

FETTUCINE WITH CHERRY TOMATOES, AVOCADO AND BACON

Preparation time: 15 minutes
Cooking time: 25 minutes
Serves 4

4 cloves garlic, unpeeled
1/3 cup (80 ml) olive oil
250 g cherry tomatoes
300 g short cut bacon (see Note)
350 g fresh fettucine
1 tablespoon white wine vinegar
2 tablespoons roughly chopped
   fresh basil
2 ripe avocados, diced
whole fresh basil leaves, to garnish

1 Preheat the oven to moderately hot 200°C (400°F/Gas 6). Place the garlic at one end of a roasting tin and drizzle with 2 tablespoons of the olive oil. Place the tomatoes at the other end and season well. Bake for 10 minutes, then remove the garlic. Return the tomatoes to the oven for a further 5–10 minutes, or until soft.
2 Cook the bacon under a hot grill for 4–5 minutes each side, or until crisp and golden. Roughly chop. Meanwhile, cook the pasta in a large saucepan of boiling water until *al dente*. Drain well and transfer to a large bowl. Drizzle 1 tablespoon of the olive oil over the pasta and toss well. Season with salt and pepper and keep warm.

3 Slit the skin of each garlic clove and squeeze the garlic out. Place in a screw-top jar with the vinegar, chopped basil and remaining oil and shake well to combine. Add the tomatoes and their juices, bacon and avocado to the fettucine, pour on the dressing and toss well. Garnish with the basil leaves and serve with a green salad and crusty bread.

NUTRITION PER SERVE
Fat 44 g; Protein 27.5 g; Carbohydrate 50.5 g; Dietary Fibre 4 g; Cholesterol 106.5 mg; 2960 kJ (705 Cal)

COOK'S FILE
Note: Short cut bacon is the meaty end of the bacon rasher and is also sold as eye bacon.

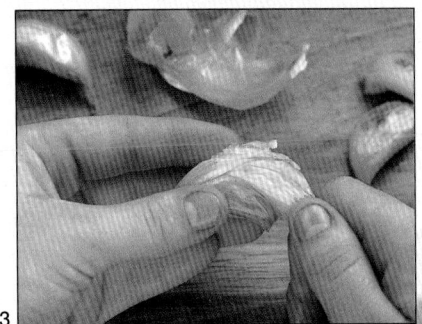

FETTUCINE WITH SWEET POTATO, FETA AND OLIVES

Preparation time: 15 minutes
Cooking time: 35 minutes
Serves 6

1.5 kg orange sweet potato, cut into 2 cm cubes
1/3 cup (80 ml) olive oil
4 cloves garlic, crushed
50 g butter
4 red onions, sliced into thin wedges
500 g fresh basil fettucine
400 g soft feta, cut into 1.5 cm cubes
200 g small black olives
1/2 cup (30 g) firmly packed fresh basil, torn

1 Preheat the oven to moderately hot 200°C (400°F/Gas 6). Place the sweet potato, oil and garlic in a bowl and toss to coat the sweet potato. Lay out the sweet potato in a roasting tin and roast for 15 minutes, then turn and return to the oven for another 15 minutes, until it is tender and golden—make sure the sweet potato is not too soft or it will not hold its shape. Set aside and keep warm.

2 Meanwhile, melt the butter in a deep frying pan and cook the onion over low heat, stirring occasionally, for 25–30 minutes, or until soft and slightly caramelised.

3 Cook the pasta in a large saucepan of boiling water until *al dente*. Drain and return to the saucepan, then add the onion and toss together. Add the sweet potato, feta, olives and basil and gently toss. Serve drizzled with extra virgin olive oil, if desired.

NUTRITION PER SERVE
Fat 32.5 g; Protein 27.5 g; Carbohydrate 90.5 g; Dietary Fibre 7 g; Cholesterol 124 mg; 3195 kJ (765 Cal)

1

2

3

BAKED BEEF VERMICELLI CAKE

Preparation time: 10 minutes +
   10 minutes standing
Cooking time: 50 minutes
Serves 4–6

80 g butter
1 onion, chopped
500 g beef mince
800 g bottled tomato pasta
   sauce
2 tablespoons tomato paste
250 g vermicelli
1/4 cup (30 g) plain flour
11/4 cups (375 ml) milk
11/4 cups (155 g) grated Cheddar

1 Preheat the oven to moderate 180°C (350°F/Gas 4). Lightly grease a 24 cm round deep springform tin. Melt 20 g of the butter in a large deep frying pan and cook the onion over medium heat for 2–3 minutes, or until soft. Add the beef mince, breaking up any lumps with the back of a spoon, and cook for 4–5 minutes, or until browned. Stir in the pasta sauce and tomato paste, reduce the heat and simmer for 20–25 minutes. Season with salt and pepper.

2 Cook the pasta in a large saucepan of boiling water until *al dente*. Drain and rinse. Meanwhile, melt the remaining butter in a saucepan over low heat. Stir in the flour and cook for 1 minute, or until pale and foaming. Remove from the heat and gradually stir in the milk. Return to the heat and stir constantly until the sauce boils and thickens. Reduce the heat and simmer for 2 minutes.

3 Spread half the pasta over the base of the tin, then cover with half the meat sauce. Cover with the remaining pasta, pressing down with the palm of your hand. Spoon on the remaining meat sauce and then pour on the white sauce. Sprinkle with cheese and cook for 15 minutes. Stand for 10 minutes before removing from the tin. Cut into wedges.

NUTRITION PER SERVE (6)
Fat 32 g; Protein 33.5 g; Carbohydrate 46.5 g; Dietary Fibre 5.5 g; Cholesterol 121 mg; 2535 kJ (605 Cal)

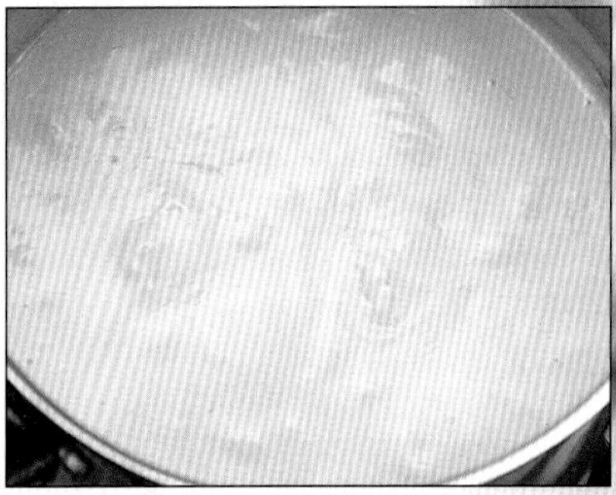

PASTA PRONTO

Preparation time: 10 minutes
Cooking time: 15 minutes
Serves 4

2 tablespoons extra virgin olive oil
4 cloves garlic, finely chopped
1 small fresh red chilli, finely
    chopped
3 x 400 g cans crushed tomatoes
1 teaspoon sugar
1/3 cup (80 ml) dry white wine
3 tablespoons chopped fresh herbs
    (e.g. basil or parsley)
400 g vermicelli
30 g shaved Parmesan

1 Heat the oil in a large deep frying pan and cook the garlic and chilli for 1 minute. Add the tomato, sugar, wine, herbs and 1¾ cups (440 ml) water. Bring to the boil and season.
2 Reduce the heat to medium and add the pasta, breaking the strands if they are too long. Cook for 10 minutes, or until the pasta is cooked, stirring often to stop the pasta from sticking. The pasta will thicken the sauce as it cooks. Season to taste and serve in bowls with shaved Parmesan.

NUTRITION PER SERVE
Fat 13.5 g; Protein 17 g; Carbohydrate 81.5 g; Dietary Fibre 9.5 g; Cholesterol 7 mg; 2225 kJ (530 Cal)

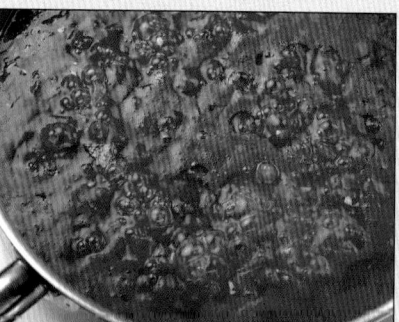

ZITI CARBONARA

Preparation time: 15 minutes
Cooking time: 15 minutes
Serves 4–6

500 g ziti
1 tablespoon olive oil
200 g piece pancetta, cut into
    long thin strips
4 egg yolks
300 ml cream
1/2 cup (50 g) grated Parmesan
2 tablespoons finely chopped
    fresh flat-leaf parsley

1 Cook the pasta in a large saucepan of boiling water until *al dente*. Drain well and return to the pan.

Meanwhile, heat the olive oil in a non-stick frying pan and cook the pancetta over high heat for 6 minutes, or until crisp and golden. **2** Beat the egg yolks, cream and Parmesan together in a bowl and season generously. Pour over the hot pasta in the saucepan and toss gently. Add the pancetta and parsley. Return the pan to very low heat and cook for 30 seconds to 1 minute, or until the sauce has thickened and coats the pasta. Don't cook over high heat or the eggs will scramble. Season with salt and pepper and serve immediately with extra Parmesan, if desired.

NUTRITION PER SERVE (6)
Fat 35.5 g; Protein 21.5 g; Carbohydrate 60 g; Dietary Fibre 4 g; Cholesterol 213.5 mg; 2700 kJ (645 Cal)

SMOKED CHICKEN LINGUINE

Preparation time: 15 minutes
Cooking time: 20 minutes
Serves 4

1 tablespoon olive oil
1 leek, thinly sliced
3 large cloves garlic, finely chopped
½ cup (125 ml) dry white wine
300 g Swiss brown mushrooms, sliced
2 teaspoons chopped fresh thyme
300 ml thick cream
2 smoked chicken breast fillets, thinly sliced (see Note)
350 g fresh linguine

1   Heat the oil in a saucepan. Add the leek and cook, stirring, over low heat for 3–4 minutes, or until soft. Add the garlic and cook for another minute. Pour in the wine and simmer for 2–3 minutes, or until the liquid has reduced by half.
2   Increase the heat to medium, add the mushrooms and thyme and cook for 5 minutes, or until any excess liquid has been absorbed, then add the cream and sliced chicken. Reduce the heat and simmer for 4–5 minutes, or until the sauce has slightly thickened. Meanwhile, cook the pasta in a large saucepan of boiling water until *al dente*. Drain and divide among serving plates. Spoon on the sauce and serve.

NUTRITION PER SERVE
Fat 39.5 g; Protein 32.5 g; Carbohydrate 52.5 g; Dietary Fibre 4 g; Cholesterol 206.5 mg; 2990 kJ (715 Cal)

COOK'S FILE
Note: You can buy smoked chicken at the deli section of some supermarkets and good delicatessens.

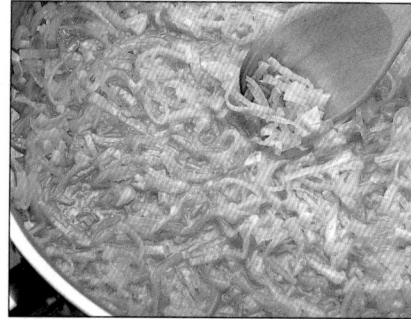

1

2

SPAGHETTINI WITH HERBS, BABY SPINACH AND GARLIC CRUMBS

Preparation time: 15 minutes
Cooking time: 15 minutes
Serves 4

375 g spaghettini
125 g day-old crusty Italian bread, crusts removed
100 ml extra virgin olive oil, plus extra for drizzling
4 cloves garlic, finely chopped
400 g baby spinach leaves
1/2 cup (25 g) chopped fresh flat-leaf parsley
4 tablespoons chopped fresh basil
1 tablespoon fresh thyme leaves
30 g shaved Parmesan

1 Cook the pasta in a large saucepan of boiling water until *al dente*. Drain, reserving 1/2 cup (125 ml) of the pasta water. Return the pasta to the saucepan and keep warm.

2 To make the garlic breadcrumbs, place the crustless bread in a food processor or blender and pulse until coarse breadcrumbs form. Heat 1 tablespoon of the oil in a saucepan. Add the breadcrumbs and half the garlic and toss for 2–3 minutes, or until lightly golden. Remove, then wipe the pan clean with paper towel.

3 Heat 2 tablespoons of the oil in the same pan. Add the spinach and remaining garlic, toss together for 1 minute, then add the herbs. Cook, tossing frequently, for a further 1 minute to wilt the herbs a little and to heat through. Toss the spinach mixture through the pasta with the remaining oil and reserved pasta water. Divide among four serving bowls and scatter with the garlic crumbs. Serve hot sprinkled with Parmesan and drizzled with extra virgin olive oil.

NUTRITION PER SERVE
Fat 23.5 g; Protein 19 g; Carbohydrate 82 g; Dietary Fibre 9 g; Cholesterol 7 mg; 2590 kJ (620 Cal)

1

2

3

AGNOLOTTI

CONCHIGLIONE

RAVIOLI

TORTELLINI

FILLED

Like a carefully chosen present, filled pasta is as good on the inside as on the outside. A delectable filling is enclosed by a pasta wrapping perfect in its simplicity.

AGNOLOTTI: The name for filled pasta in the Piedmont region of Italy, agnolotti can be shaped into squares, crescents or circles, and usually have ruffled edges. Agnolotti was originally used to wrap up leftovers of meat and sausage in fresh pasta.

Chicken agnolotti: Pasta filled with chicken mince, often combined with cheese, spinach or another meat. Any other chicken-filled pasta can be used instead.

Ricotta agnolotti: The ricotta filling is the same as that used in ravioli and tortellini and the three shapes are interchangeable.

Veal agnolotti: Meat is the most common filling for agnolotti—predominantly veal combined with other meats. These can be substituted with other pasta shapes filled with veal, such as ravioli or tortellini. The best sauce for veal-filled pastas is a simple cream, cheese or butter-based sauce that does not compete with the flavours of the filling.

CONCHIGLIONE (large shells): Part of the conchiglie (shell) family of pasta (see page 7 for more information), conchiglione is the largest of the shells. It is usually stuffed with a filling and baked in a ceramic dish: its shape makes it a natural for stuffing as the hollow centre is excellent for holding cheese, meat or seafood and sauce. It can be substituted with other large pasta shapes including large rigatoni (page 7) or lumaconi, the giant pasta snails (not shown).

RAVIOLI: The most recognised filled pasta outside Italy, ravioli are little stuffed square pasta pillows.

Chicken ravioli: Chicken ravioli are usually made out of a mixture of chicken, cheese and either a meat such as pork or prosciutto, or with the addition of spinach. You can use another chicken-filled pasta instead.

Ricotta ravioli: The simple ricotta filling makes this a very versatile pasta suitable for many different flavoured sauces. The filling will sometimes be wrapped in plain pasta and sometimes with a flavoured pasta, such as spinach. Any ricotta-filled pasta will work just as well.

Seafood ravioli: A variety of seafood can be used to fill ravioli, including fish, smoked salmon and crustaceans. Small seafood such as prawns and scallops are ideal fillings as their texture and flavour are well matched to being encased in pasta, cooked quickly and dressed with oil or butter and herbs or creamy sauces. Usually only available at pasta shops or delicatessens.

Spinach ravioli: Ravioli with ricotta and spinach is known as 'di magro' in Italian, meaning lean. To make this favourite filling, spinach is combined with ricotta, Parmesan and nutmeg. It can be replaced with spinach tortellini or agnolotti.

Veal ravioli: A filling of veal mixed with minced pork, Parmesan and nutmeg is excellent served with a herb-flavoured butter. Replace with another veal-filled pasta.

TORTELLINI: Originating in Bologna, these small pasta rings are said to be named after Venus' navel. There are several popular fillings.

Cheese tortellini: Cheese is by far the most widely available and simplest filling for tortellini. The usual cheese filling is made up of a mixture of ricotta with a small amount of Parmesan, but a range of other cheeses can be used instead, including provolone, Gruyère, goat's cheese and fontina. Cheese tortellini can be replaced with cheese ravioli or agnolotti.

Ham and cheese tortellini: Using the classic combination of ham and cheese, this is a perennial favourite. The mixture of cooked ham, Parmesan, nutmeg and fresh herbs is well suited to a herb-flavoured butter sauce. Mortadella or Italian sausage are sometimes used as a variation to the ham. Substitute other pastas with the same filling.

Veal tortellini: The filling is usually made up of predominantly veal mixed with other meats (for example, pork, mortadella and prosciutto). Sometimes Parmesan and spices, such as nutmeg, are added to the mixture. Traditionally these little pasta crescents are served in Bologna's speciality 'tortellini in brodo', which is in consommé, or with melted butter and cheese. Other veal-filled pastas can be used instead.

VEAL AGNOLOTTI WITH ALFREDO SAUCE

Preparation time: 10 minutes
Cooking time: 10 minutes
Serves 4–6

625 g veal agnolotti
90 g butter
1 1/2 cups (150 g) grated Parmesan
300 ml cream
2 tablespoons chopped fresh
   marjoram

1 Cook the pasta in a large saucepan of boiling water until *al dente*. Drain and return to the pan.
2 Just before the pasta is cooked, melt the butter in a saucepan over low heat. Add the Parmesan and cream and bring to the boil. Reduce the heat and simmer, stirring constantly, for 2 minutes, or until the sauce has thickened slightly. Stir in the marjoram and season with salt and cracked black pepper. Toss the sauce through the pasta until well coated and serve immediately.

NUTRITION PER SERVE (6)
Fat 48.5 g; Protein 21.5 g; Carbohydrate 39.5 g; Dietary Fibre 3.5 g; Cholesterol 156.5 mg; 2835 kJ (680 Cal)

COOK'S FILE
Variation: Marjoram can be replaced with any other fresh herb you prefer—for example, try parsley, thyme, chervil or dill.

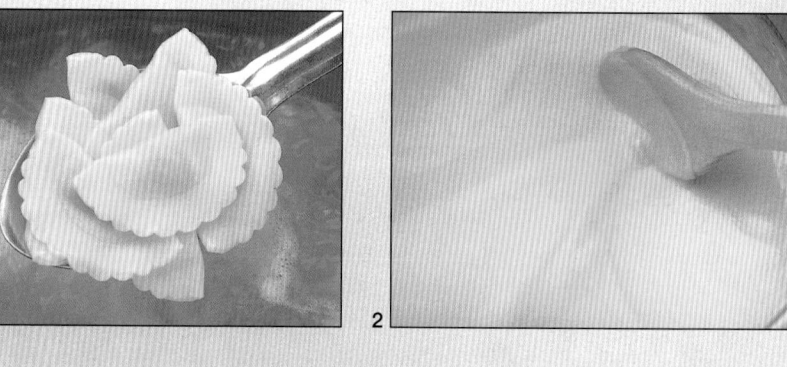

RAVIOLI WITH PRAWNS AND KAFFIR LIME SAUCE

Preparation time: 15 minutes
Cooking time: 20 minutes
Serves 4

50 g butter
4 cloves garlic, crushed
750 g medium raw prawns, peeled and deveined
1½ tablespoons plain flour
1½ cups (375 ml) fish stock
2 cups (500 ml) cream
5 kaffir lime leaves, shredded
625 g seafood ravioli (see Note)
3 teaspoons fish sauce

1 Melt the butter in a deep large frying pan and cook the garlic over medium heat for 1 minute. Add the prawns and cook for 3–4 minutes, or until they turn pink and are cooked through. Remove from the pan, leaving any juices in the pan. Add the flour and stir for 1 minute, or until light golden. Gradually stir in the stock, then add the cream and kaffir lime leaves. Reduce the heat and simmer for 10 minutes, or until slightly thickened.

2 Meanwhile, cook the pasta in a large saucepan of boiling water until *al dente*. Drain. Stir the fish sauce through the cream sauce, add the prawns and stir until warmed through. Divide the pasta among four warm serving plates and spoon on the prawns and sauce. Season to taste with salt and cracked black pepper and serve immediately.

NUTRITION PER SERVE
Fat 75.5 g; Protein 42 g; Carbohydrate 62.5 g; Dietary Fibre 5.5 g; Cholesterol 428.5 mg; 4575 kJ (1095 Cal)

COOK'S FILE
Note: Seafood ravioli is available from speciality pasta shops, but if it is unavailable, you can use ricotta ravioli instead—the flavours work well.

SALMON AND RICOTTA-STUFFED CONCHIGLIONE

Preparation time: 15 minutes
Cooking time: 40 minutes
Serves 4

200 g (about 32) conchiglione
   (large shells)
425 g can good-quality red salmon,
   drained, bones removed, flaked
500 g fresh ricotta
1 tablespoon chopped fresh flat-leaf
   parsley
3 tablespoons chopped fresh chives
1 1/2 celery sticks, finely chopped
3/4 cup (90 g) grated Cheddar
3/4 cup (185 ml) cream
1/4 cup (25 g) grated Parmesan

1 Preheat the oven to moderate 180°C (350°F/Gas 4). Cook the pasta in a large saucepan of boiling water for 4–5 minutes. Drain.
2 Combine the salmon, ricotta, parsley, chives, celery and Cheddar in a bowl and season to taste with salt and cracked black pepper.
3 Place 2 teaspoons of filling in each shell and transfer the filled shells to a 3 litre 26 x 36 cm (7 cm deep) ceramic baking dish. Once they are all in the dish, pour on the cream and sprinkle with Parmesan. Cover with foil and bake for 20 minutes, then remove the foil and return to the oven for 15 minutes, or until golden brown. Serve in pasta bowls with the sauce spooned over the shells.

NUTRITION PER SERVE (6)
Fat 35.5 g; Protein 31 g; Carbohydrate 37.5 g; Dietary Fibre 3 g; Cholesterol 135 mg; 2470 kJ (590 Cal)

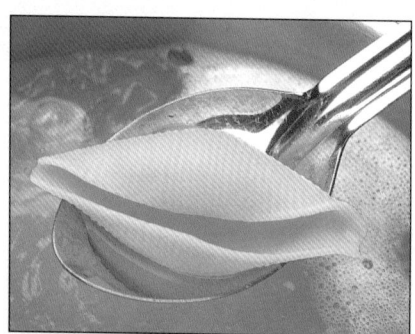
1

2

3

SPINACH RAVIOLI WITH ROASTED TOMATOES AND GOAT'S CHEESE

Preparation time: 15 minutes
Cooking time: 1 hour
Serves 4

4 Roma tomatoes
6 cloves garlic, unpeeled and bruised
1/3 cup (80 ml) extra virgin olive oil
2 1/2 teaspoons caster sugar
500 g spinach ravioli
2 tablespoons red wine vinegar
90 g pitted Kalamata olives
100 g baby spinach leaves
100 g goat's cheese, crumbled

1 Preheat the oven to moderately hot 190°C (375°F/Gas 5). Cut the tomatoes into quarters, then cut each quarter in half. Place the tomatoes on a large lightly greased baking tray, along with the bruised garlic cloves.

Drizzle with 1 tablespoon of the olive oil, then sprinkle with 1 teaspoon of the sugar. Season with salt and black pepper. Roast for 1 hour, or until softened and caramelised. Remove and keep warm.

2 Just before the tomatoes are ready, cook the pasta in a large saucepan of boiling water until *al dente*. Drain and place in a large bowl. Remove the skins from the garlic.

3 To make the dressing, combine the remaining extra virgin olive oil with the red wine vinegar, roasted garlic and the remaining sugar in a screw-top jar and shake until well combined. Pour over the pasta and toss gently. Add the olives, baby spinach leaves, goat's cheese and roasted tomato and toss together. Serve immediately.

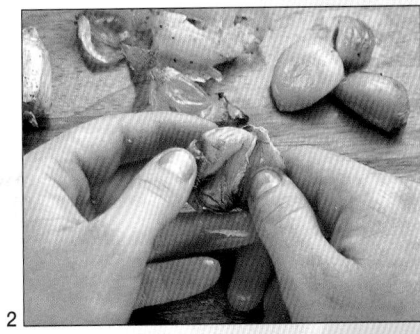

NUTRITION PER SERVE
Fat 25 g; Protein 14.5 g; Carbohydrate 39.5 g; Dietary Fibre 6 g; Cholesterol 29.5 mg; 1850 kJ (440 Cal)

CHICKEN RAVIOLI WITH PESTO

Preparation time: 10 minutes
Cooking time: 10 minutes
Serves 4

625 g chicken ravioli
1 cup (50 g) firmly packed fresh basil
2 cloves garlic, peeled
1/4 cup (40 g) pine nuts, toasted
1/2 cup (125 ml) extra virgin olive oil
1/2 cup (50 g) grated Parmesan
50 g pecorino cheese, grated
1/4 cup (15 g) firmly packed fresh basil, extra, torn
30 g shaved Parmesan, to serve

1 Cook the pasta in a large saucepan of boiling water until *al dente*. Meanwhile, blend the basil, garlic, pine nuts and olive oil in a food processor or blender until smooth. Stir in the grated Parmesan and pecorino and season to taste with salt and pepper.
2 Drain the pasta, reserving 1 tablespoon of the cooking water to add to the pesto. Carefully toss the ravioli in the pesto and reserved water and finish with a drizzle of extra virgin olive oil, a little torn basil and some Parmesan shavings.

NUTRITION PER SERVE
Fat 54 g; Protein 30 g; Carbohydrate 57.5 g; Dietary Fibre 6.5 g; Cholesterol 83 mg; 3490 kJ (835 Cal)

1

2

PASTA WITH CREAMY SEMI-DRIED TOMATO SAUCE AND BACON

Preparation time: 10 minutes
Cooking time: 20 minutes
Serves 4

4 rashers bacon
625 g veal or chicken agnolotti
1 tablespoon olive oil
2 cloves garlic, finely chopped
2/3 cup (110 g) thinly sliced semi-
   dried tomatoes
1 tablespoon chopped fresh thyme

1 1/2 cups (375 ml) cream
1 teaspoon finely grated lemon rind
1/3 cup (35 g) finely grated Parmesan

1 Grill the bacon for 5 minutes each side, or until crisp and golden. Remove, drain well on paper towel, then break into pieces.

2 Cook the pasta in a large saucepan of boiling water until *al dente*. Drain and keep warm. Heat the oil in a frying pan and cook the garlic over medium heat for 1 minute, or until just golden. Add the semi-dried tomatoes and thyme and cook for 1 minute more.

3 Add the cream, bring to the boil, then reduce the heat and simmer for 6–8 minutes, or until the cream has thickened and reduced by one third. Season with salt and pepper, add the lemon rind and 2 tablespoons of the Parmesan. Divide the pasta among four serving bowls and pour on the sauce. Sprinkle with the remaining Parmesan and the bacon pieces. Serve immediately.

NUTRITION PER SERVE
Fat 60.5 g; Protein 32 g; Carbohydrate 64.5 g; Dietary Fibre 7.5 g; Cholesterol 212 mg; 3895 kJ (930 Cal)

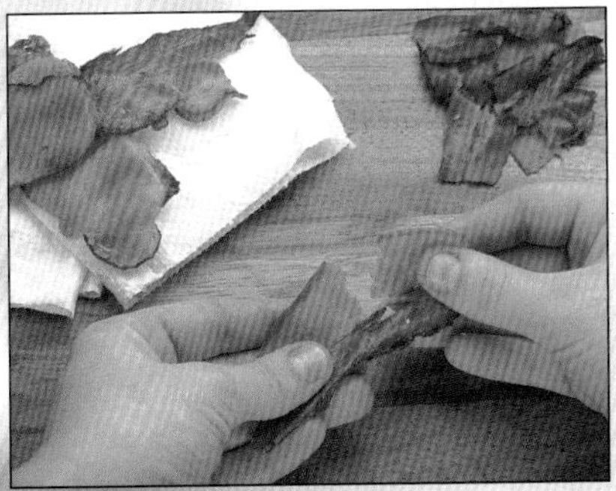

VEAL RAVIOLI WITH HERB BUTTER

Preparation time: 10 minutes
Cooking time: 10 minutes
Serves 4

500 g good-quality veal ravioli
100 g butter, softened
3 cloves garlic, crushed
2 tablespoons finely chopped fresh
   flat-leaf parsley
2 teaspoons finely chopped fresh
   sage
2 teaspoons chopped fresh thyme
1/4 cup (60 ml) white wine
1 large vine-ripened tomato,
   finely diced

1 Cook the pasta in a large saucepan of boiling water until *al dente*. Drain, return to the pan and keep warm.
2 Meanwhile, melt the butter in a large frying pan over medium heat. Add the garlic and herbs and cook, stirring, for 1 minute. Add the wine and cook for another minute. Pour over the pasta, add the tomato and toss over medium heat until warmed through. Divide among four serving plates and serve.

NUTRITION PER SERVE
Fat 29 g; Protein 14 g; Carbohydrate 46.5 g; Dietary Fibre 5.5 g; Cholesterol 96 mg; 2140 kJ (510 Cal)

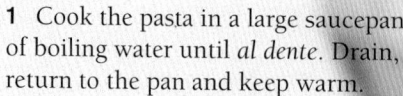

RICOTTA AND PROSCIUTTO-FILLED CONCHIGLIONE

Preparation time: 15 minutes
Cooking time: 40 minutes
Serves 4–6

24 conchiglione (large shells)
200 g prosciutto, roughly chopped
2 tablespoons chopped fresh chives
1 cup (60 g) chopped fresh basil
80 g butter
500 g fresh ricotta
1 cup (150 g) chopped sun-dried
    capsicum

1 cup (100 g) grated Parmesan
3 cups (750 g) bottled tomato pasta
    sauce

1 Preheat the oven to moderate 180°C (350°F/Gas 4). Cook the pasta in a large saucepan of boiling water until *al dente*. Drain. Place the prosciutto, chives and basil in a food processor or blender and pulse until chopped.
2 Melt the butter in large frying pan over medium heat. Add the prosciutto mixture and cook for about 5 minutes, or until the prosciutto is golden and crisp. Transfer the mixture to a bowl, add

the ricotta, capsicum and ¹/4 cup (25 g) of the Parmesan. Stir well. Season to taste with salt and cracked black pepper.
3 Pour the pasta sauce into a 3 litre ovenproof ceramic baking dish. Spoon the ricotta mixture into the pasta shells and place into the baking dish. Sprinkle the remaining Parmesan over the shells and bake for 25–30 minutes, or until the top of the shells turn golden. Spoon the sauce over the shells and serve.

NUTRITION PER SERVE (6)
Fat 28 g; Protein 27 g; Carbohydrate 31.5 g; Dietary Fibre 4.5 g; Cholesterol 107 mg; 2040 kJ (485 Cal)

1

2

3

RAVIOLI WITH ROASTED RED CAPSICUM SAUCE

Preparation time: 15 minutes
Cooking time: 15 minutes
Serves 4

6 red capsicums
6 slices prosciutto
625 g chicken or ricotta ravioli
2 tablespoons olive oil
3 cloves garlic, crushed
2 leeks, thinly sliced
1 tablespoon chopped fresh oregano
2 teaspoons soft brown sugar
1 cup (250 ml) hot chicken stock

1 Cut the capsicums into large pieces, removing the seeds and membrane. Place, skin-side-up, under a hot grill until the skin blackens and blisters. Cool in a plastic bag, then peel away the skin. Place the prosciutto under the hot grill and cook for 1 minute each side, or until crisp. Break into pieces and set aside.

2 Cook the pasta in a large saucepan of boiling water until *al dente*. Meanwhile, heat the oil in a frying pan and cook the garlic and leek over medium heat for 3–4 minutes, or until softened. Add the oregano and sugar and stir for 1 minute.

3 Place the capsicum and leek mixture in a food processor or blender, season with salt and pepper and process until combined. Add the chicken stock and process until smooth. Drain the pasta and return to the saucepan. Gently toss the sauce through the ravioli over low heat until warmed through. Divide among four serving bowls and sprinkle with prosciutto.

NUTRITION PER SERVE
Fat 20 g; Protein 25 g; Carbohydrate 59 g;
Dietary Fibre 8.5 g; Cholesterol 56.5 mg;
2150 kJ (515 Cal)

HAM TORTELLINI WITH NUTTY HERB SAUCE

Preparation time: 15 minutes
Cooking time: 10 minutes
Serves 4–6

500 g ham and cheese tortellini
60 g butter
1 cup (100 g) walnuts, chopped
2/3 cup (100 g) pine nuts
2 tablespoons finely chopped fresh
    flat-leaf parsley
2 teaspoons chopped fresh thyme
1/4 cup (60 g) fresh ricotta
1/4 cup (60 ml) thick cream

1 Cook the pasta in a large saucepan of boiling water until *al dente*. Drain and return to the pan. Meanwhile, heat the butter in a frying pan over medium heat until foaming. Add the walnuts and pine nuts and stir for 5 minutes, or until golden brown. Add the parsley and thyme and season to taste.

2 Beat the ricotta and cream together. Add the nutty sauce to the pasta and toss. Divide among serving bowls and top with the ricotta cream.

NUTRITION PER SERVE (6)
Fat 47 g; Protein 21.5 g; Carbohydrate 23 g; Dietary Fibre 3.5 g; Cholesterol 84.5 mg; 2495 kJ (595 Cal)

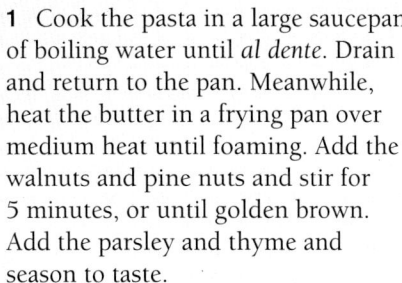

LASAGNE

LASAGNETTE

PAPPARDELLE

STRACCI

FLAT

Not content to be the poor relation, flat pasta makes its biggest impact by layering sheets of pasta with a delicious filling. Lasagne is always a favourite, but it is only one of many mouth-watering options using flat pasta.

LASAGNE: The name lasagne refers to the pasta sheet, not the meal of the same name.

Dried lasagne: Dried lasagne sheets are readily available from the supermarket and are best cooked as their packet instructions indicate. These large sheets of dried pasta are used for making baked, layered pasta dishes and are increasingly being used for free-form pasta stacks.

Fresh lasagne: The starting point for all fresh pasta, lasagne sheets are traditionally used for layered, baked pasta dishes. Fresh sheets are available from some supermarkets and delicatessens. Originating from Emilia–Romana (an area in northern Italy), the classic baked dish *al forno* is still the most popularly known lasagne dish with layers of lasagne sheets, a rich meat ragout and béchamel sauce with a topping of Parmesan. Other regions of Italy have their own variations of lasagne, featuring seafood, vegetables, cured meats and sausages. Lasagne sheets can also be used to make home-made ravioli and free-form lasagne, where the cooked sheets are layered with a filling just before being served. There is no satisfactory substitute for lasagne.

LASAGNETTE: Also called mafalde or mafaldini, these wide, long fluted lengths of pasta have slightly crimped edges ideal for catching their accompanying sauce. Lasagnette is best matched with rich meat, vegetable, cream or cheese sauces. It is usually available dried, not fresh. If you can't find it, use another dried pasta of a similar length and width, such as pappardelle.

PAPPARDELLE: This pasta derives its name from the verb *pappare*, meaning 'to gobble up' in Italian.

Dried pappardelle: These dried, very wide pasta ribbons are different to most other dried pastas as their dough is enriched with eggs, which is quite unusual for a dried pasta. Their width and length are best matched with strong sauces that will cover their entire surface area. You can replace dried pappardelle with dried tagliatelle (page 47) or lasagnette, but unless you are using an egg pasta, they will not have quite the same flavour.

Fresh pappardelle: Fresh pappardelle is a wide ribbon-shaped egg noodle pasta, 20–30 cm long and 3–5 cm wide. Shorter and wider than tagliatelle, pappardelle is the traditional companion to rich game sauces such as hare. It suits sauces made with other gamey meats like rabbit, strong vegetables like fennel or raddichio and creamy sauces. If necessary, you can replace fresh pappardelle with fresh fettucine, tagliatelle (page 47) or lasagnette.

STRACCI: Made from fresh pasta sheets, stracci, meaning 'stretched' in Italian, is one of the easiest pasta shapes to make. Large pasta sheets are simply sliced into reasonably large and varied shapes by cutting different lengths along a range of angles. Stracci can be substituted quite easily by breaking dried lasagne sheets into ragged pieces measuring about 7 cm x 12 cm. Any sauce that goes with stracci will also go well with fresh or dried fettucine or tagliatelle (page 47). Stracci is most often available dried.

SMOKED SALMON STRACCI IN CHAMPAGNE SAUCE

Preparation time: 15 minutes
Cooking time: 10 minutes
Serves 4

375 g fresh stracci
1 tablespoon olive oil
2 large cloves garlic, crushed
1/2 cup (125 ml) Champagne
1 cup (250 ml) thick cream

200 g smoked salmon, cut into thin strips
2 tablespoons small capers in brine, rinsed, patted dry
2 tablespoons chopped fresh chives
2 tablespoons chopped fresh dill

1 Cook the pasta in a large saucepan of boiling water until *al dente*. Drain and return to the pan. Meanwhile, heat the oil in a large frying pan and cook the garlic over medium heat for 30 seconds. Pour in the Champagne and cook for 2–3 minutes, or until reduced slightly. Add the cream and cook for 3–4 minutes, or until reduced and thickened.

2 Add the sauce and remaining ingredients to the hot pasta and toss gently. Season to taste with salt and cracked black pepper and serve immediately.

NUTRITION PER SERVE
Fat 32.5 g; Protein 23.5 g; Carbohydrate 54.5 g; Dietary Fibre 1.5 g; Cholesterol 164.5 mg; 2600 kJ (620 Cal)

PAPPARDELLE WITH BUG TAIL AND SAFFRON CREAM SAUCE

Preparation time: 10 minutes
Cooking time: 20 minutes
Serves 4–6

400 g pappardelle
60 g butter
4 large cloves garlic, crushed
250 g Swiss brown mushrooms,
   sliced
500 g fresh or frozen raw bug meat
   or lobster tail meat

½ cup (125 ml) white wine
½ teaspoon saffron threads
700 ml thick cream
2 egg yolks

1 Cook the pasta in a large saucepan of boiling water until *al dente*. Meanwhile, melt the butter in a large deep frying pan, add the garlic and mushrooms and cook over medium heat for 2–3 minutes, or until soft. Add the bug meat and cook for 4–5 minutes, or until just cooked through. Remove from the pan.
2 Add the wine and saffron to the pan, scraping the bottom to remove any sediment. Bring to the boil and cook for 2–3 minutes, or until reduced. Add the cream, reduce the heat and simmer for 5 minutes. Whisk through the egg yolks until thickened. Return the bug meat mixture to the pan and stir until warmed through. Drain the pasta and divide among serving dishes. Spoon on the bug meat sauce and season to taste with salt and cracked black pepper. Serve immediately.

NUTRITION PER SERVE (6)
Fat 54.5 g; Protein 28.5 g; Carbohydrate 51.5 g; Dietary Fibre 3 g; Cholesterol 308.5 mg; 3430 kJ (820 Cal)

BLUE CHEESE AND WALNUT LASAGNETTE

Preparation time: 10 minutes
Cooking time: 15 minutes
Serves 4

375 g lasagnette
1 cup (100 g) walnuts
40 g butter
3 French shallots, finely chopped
1 tablespoon brandy or cognac
1 cup (250 ml) crème fraîche
200 g gorgonzola cheese, crumbled
75 g baby spinach leaves

1 Preheat the oven to moderately hot 200°C (400°F/Gas 6). Cook the pasta in a large saucepan of boiling water until *al dente*. Drain, return to the pan and keep warm. Meanwhile, place the walnuts on a baking tray and roast for 5 minutes, or until golden and toasted. Cool, then roughly chop.

2 Heat the butter in a large saucepan, add the shallots and cook over medium heat for 1–2 minutes, or until soft, taking care not to brown. Add the brandy and simmer for 1 minute, then stir in the crème fraîche and gorgonzola. Cook for 3–4 minutes, or until the cheese has melted and the sauce has thickened. Stir in the spinach and toasted walnuts, reserving 1 tablespoon for garnish. Heat gently until the spinach has just wilted. Season with salt and cracked black pepper. Gently mix the sauce through the pasta. Divide among serving plates and sprinkle with the reserved walnuts.

NUTRITION PER SERVE
Fat 63.5 g; Protein 31.5 g; Carbohydrate 68.5 g; Dietary Fibre 4.5 g; Cholesterol 152 mg; 4095 kJ (980 Cal)

COOK'S FILE
Note: The gorgonzola needs to be young as this gives a sweeter, milder flavour.

PAPPARDELLE WITH SALAMI, LEEK AND PROVOLONE CHEESE

Preparation time: 15 minutes
Cooking time: 15 minutes
Serves 4

375 g pappardelle
2 tablespoons olive oil
2 leeks, thinly sliced (including some of the green section)
2 tablespoons white wine
2 x 400 g cans diced tomatoes
150 g sliced mild salami, cut into strips
¼ cup (7 g) fresh basil leaves, torn
125 g provolone cheese, sliced into 3 cm wide strips
30 g grated Parmesan

1 Cook the pasta in a large saucepan of boiling water until *al dente*, then drain and return to the pan. Meanwhile, heat the olive oil in a large deep frying pan, add the leek and cook over low heat for 4 minutes, or until soft but not browned. Increase the heat to medium, add the wine and stir until almost evaporated.

2 Add the tomato and salami, season with salt and cracked black pepper and simmer for 5 minutes, or until reduced slightly. Toss the tomato sauce mixture, basil and provolone lightly through the pasta. Sprinkle with Parmesan and serve.

NUTRITION PER SERVE
Fat 37 g; Protein 34 g; Carbohydrate 74.5 g; Dietary Fibre 6 g; Cholesterol 94 mg; 3250 kJ (775 Cal)

1

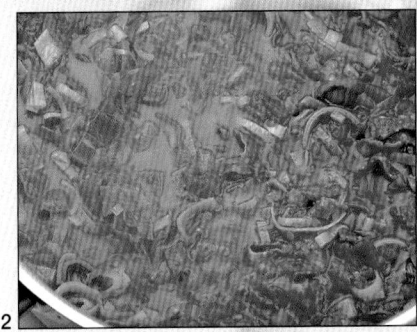

2

BOCCONCINI, PROSCIUTTO AND SPINACH LASAGNE

Preparation time: 15 minutes +
10 minutes standing
Cooking time: 25 minutes
Serves 4–6

600 g bottled tomato pasta sauce
250 g fresh lasagne sheets
400 g bocconcini, thinly sliced
500 g English spinach, trimmed
1/2 cup (125 ml) cream
10 thin slices prosciutto, chopped
1 cup (150 g) grated mozzarella
cheese
1/2 cup (50 g) finely grated Parmesan

1 Preheat the oven to moderate 180°C (350°F/Gas 4). Lightly grease a 3 litre shallow 22 cm x 30 cm ovenproof dish. Spread half of the tomato pasta sauce over the base of the dish. Cover the layer of pasta sauce with a third of the lasagne sheets. Top with half of the bocconcini and half of the spinach. Drizzle on half of the cream and sprinkle with half of the prosciutto. Season with some salt and cracked black pepper. Repeat to give two layers, starting with half of the remaining lasagne sheets.

2 Lay the final layer of lasagne over the top and spread with the remaining pasta sauce. Sprinkle with the combined mozzarella and Parmesan. Bake for 25 minutes, or until cooked. Leave to stand for 10 minutes before serving.

NUTRITION PER SERVE (6)
Fat 29.5 g; Protein 35 g; Carbohydrate 30.5 g; Dietary Fibre 4.5 g; Cholesterol 120.5 mg; 2200 kJ (525 Cal)

ROAST PUMPKIN SAUCE ON PAPPARDELLE

Preparation time: 15 minutes
Cooking time: 35 minutes
Serves 4

1.4 kg butternut pumpkin, cut into
    2 cm pieces
4 cloves garlic, crushed
3 teaspoons fresh thyme leaves
100 ml olive oil
500 g pappardelle
2 tablespoons cream
3/4 cup (185 ml) hot chicken stock
30 g shaved Parmesan

1 Preheat the oven to moderately hot 200°C (400°F/Gas 6). Place the pumpkin, garlic, thyme and 1/4 cup (60 ml) of the olive oil in a bowl and toss together. Season with salt, transfer to a baking tray and cook for 30 minutes, or until tender and golden. Meanwhile, cook the pasta in a large saucepan of boiling water until *al dente*. Drain and return to the pan. Toss through the remaining oil and keep warm.

2 Place the cooked pumpkin and the cream in a food processor or blender and process until smooth. Add the hot stock and process until smooth and combined. Season with salt and cracked black pepper and gently toss through the warm pasta. Divide among four serving plates, sprinkle with Parmesan and extra thyme leaves, if desired, and serve immediately.

NUTRITION PER SERVE
Fat 29.5 g; Protein 26 g; Carbohydrate 109.5 g; Dietary Fibre 7.5 g; Cholesterol 43 mg; 3400 kJ (810 Cal)

COOK'S FILE
Note: The sauce becomes gluggy on standing, so serve it as soon as possible.

FREE-FORM WILD MUSHROOM LASAGNE

Preparation time: 10 minutes +
   15 minutes soaking
Cooking time: 15 minutes
Serves 4

10 g dried porcini mushrooms
350 g assorted wild mushrooms
   (shiitake, oyster, Swiss brown)
30 g butter
1 small onion, halved and thinly sliced
1 tablespoon chopped fresh thyme
3 egg yolks
1/2 cup (125 ml) thick cream
1 cup (100 g) grated Parmesan
8 fresh lasagne sheets (10 x 25 cm)

1 Soak the porcini in 1/4 cup (60 ml) boiling water for 15 minutes. Strain through a sieve, reserving the liquid. Cut the larger of all the mushrooms in half. Heat the butter in a frying pan and cook the onion over medium heat for 1–2 minutes, or until just soft. Add the thyme and mushrooms (including the porcini) and cook for 1–2 minutes, or until softened. Pour in the reserved mushroom liquid and cook for 1–2 minutes, or until the liquid has evaporated. Set aside.

2 Beat the egg yolks, cream and half the Parmesan in a large bowl. Cook the lasagne sheets in a large saucepan of boiling water for 2–3 minutes, stirring gently. Drain well and toss the sheets gently through the egg mixture while hot. Reheat the mushrooms quickly. To serve, place a sheet of folded lasagne on a plate, top with some mushrooms, then another sheet of folded lasagne. Drizzle with any remaining egg mixture and sprinkle with the remaining Parmesan.

NUTRITION PER SERVE
Fat 30 g; Protein 20 g; Carbohydrate 30 g; Dietary Fibre 4.5 g; Cholesterol 213 mg; 1950 kJ (465 Cal)

CREAMY CHICKEN AND PEPPERCORN PAPPARDELLE

Preparation time: 15 minutes
Cooking time: 15 minutes
Serves 4

2 chicken breast fillets (420 g in total)
30 g butter
1 onion, halved and thinly sliced
2 tablespoons drained green
   peppercorns, slightly crushed
1/2 cup (125 ml) white wine
300 ml cream

400 g fresh pappardelle
1/3 cup (80 g) sour cream (optional)
2 tablespoons chopped fresh chives

1 Cut the chicken in half so that you have four flat fillets and season with salt and pepper. Melt the butter in a frying pan, add the chicken and cook for 3 minutes each side, or until lightly browned and cooked through. Remove from the pan, cut into slices and keep warm.

2 Add the onion and peppercorns to the same pan and cook over medium heat for 3 minutes, or until the onion has softened slightly. Add the wine and cook for 1 minute, or until reduced by half. Stir in the cream and cook for 4–5 minutes, or until thickened slightly, then season with salt and pepper. Meanwhile, cook the pasta in a large saucepan of boiling water until *al dente*, then drain. Mix together the pasta, chicken and any juices and cream sauce. Divide the pasta among serving bowls, top with a dollop of sour cream and sprinkle with chives.

NUTRITION PER SERVE
Fat 50 g; Protein 37.5 g; Carbohydrate 59.5 g; Dietary Fibre 1.5 g; Cholesterol 250 mg; 3580 kJ (855 Cal)

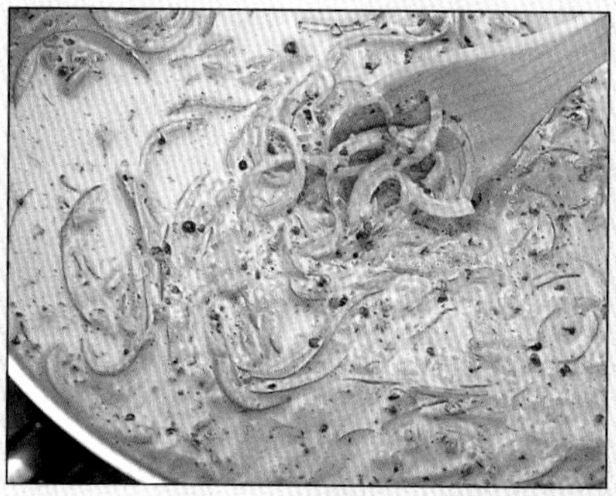

LASAGNETTE WITH SPICY CHICKEN MEATBALLS

Preparation time: 10 minutes
Cooking time: 15 minutes
Serves 4

750 g chicken mince
2 tablespoons chopped fresh
   coriander leaves
1½ tablespoons red curry paste
2 tablespoons oil
1 red onion, finely chopped
3 cloves garlic, crushed

3½ cups (875 g) tomato pasta sauce
2 teaspoons soft brown sugar
350 g lasagnette

1 Line a tray with baking paper. Combine the mince, coriander and 1 tablespoon of the curry paste in a bowl. Roll heaped tablespoons of the mixture into balls and put on the tray—you should get about 20 balls. Refrigerate until ready to use.
2 Heat the oil in a large deep frying pan and cook the onion and garlic over medium heat for 2–3 minutes, or until softened. Add the remaining curry paste and cook, stirring, for

1 minute, or until fragrant. Add the pasta sauce and sugar and stir well. Reduce the heat, add the meatballs and cook, turning halfway through, for 10 minutes, or until the meatballs are cooked through.
3 Meanwhile, cook the pasta in a large saucepan of boiling water until *al dente*. Drain and divide among four serving bowls. Top with the sauce and meatballs and sprinkle with fresh coriander, if desired.

NUTRITION PER SERVE
Fat 29 g; Protein 51.5 g; Carbohydrate 79 g; Dietary Fibre 8.5 g; Cholesterol 184.5 mg; 3300 kJ (790 Cal)

1

2

3

FREE-FORM PUMPKIN, SPINACH AND RICOTTA LASAGNE

Preparation time: 15 minutes
Cooking time: 15 minutes
Serves 4

1/4 cup (60 ml) olive oil
1.5 kg butternut pumpkin, cut
    into 1.5 cm dice
500 g English spinach leaves,
    thoroughly washed
4 fresh lasagne sheets (12 cm x
    20 cm)
2 cups (500 g) fresh ricotta
2 tablespoons cream
1/4 cup (25 g) grated Parmesan
pinch ground nutmeg

1 Heat the oil in a large non-stick frying pan over medium heat. Add the pumpkin and toss together. Cook, stirring occasionally, for 15 minutes, or until tender (don't worry if the pumpkin is slightly mashed). Season and keep warm.
2 Meanwhile, cook the spinach in a large saucepan of boiling water for 30 seconds, or until wilted. Using a slotted spoon, transfer the spinach to a bowl of cold water. Drain well and squeeze out as much excess water as possible. Finely chop the spinach. Add the lasagne sheets to the saucepan of boiling water and cook, stirring occasionally, until *al dente*. Drain and lay the lasagne sheets side-by-side on a clean tea towel. Cut each sheet widthways into thirds.
3 Combine the ricotta, cream, Parmesan, chopped spinach and nutmeg in a small saucepan and stir over low heat for 2–3 minutes, or until warmed through. Work quickly to assemble. Place a piece of lasagne on the base of each plate. Using half the pumpkin, top each of the sheets, then cover with another lasagne piece. Use half the ricotta mixture to spread over the lasagne sheets then add another lasagne piece. Top with the remaining pumpkin, then the remaining ricotta mixture. Season and serve immediately.

NUTRITION PER SERVE
Fat 34.5 g; Protein 27.5 g; Carbohydrate 40 g;
Dietary Fibre 8 g; Cholesterol 79.5 mg;
2425 kJ (580 Cal)

1

2

3

CHINESE ROAST DUCK WITH FRESH PAPPARDELLE

Preparation time: 15 minutes
Cooking time: 10 minutes
Serves 4–6

250 g baby bok choy, washed and
    leaves separated
600 g fresh pappardelle
1 Chinese roast duck, skin removed
    (see Note)
1/3 cup (80 ml) peanut oil
3 cloves garlic, crushed
3 teaspoons finely chopped fresh
    ginger
3/4 cup (35 g) chopped fresh
    coriander leaves
2 tablespoons hoisin sauce
2 tablespoons oyster sauce

1 Bring a large saucepan of water to the boil and blanch the bok choy for 1–2 minutes, or until tender, but still crisp. Remove with a slotted spoon and keep warm. In the same pan of boiling water, cook the pasta until *al dente*. Drain well and keep warm.
2 Remove the duck meat from the bones and finely shred. Heat the peanut oil in a small saucepan over high heat and bring it up to smoking point. Remove from the heat and allow to cool for 1 minute, then swirl in the garlic and ginger to infuse the oil. Be careful not to allow the garlic to burn or it will turn bitter.
3 Pour the hot oil over the pasta and add the bok choy, duck, coriander, hoisin and oyster sauces. Toss well, season and serve immediately.

NUTRITION PER SERVE (6)
Fat 19.5 g; Protein 29 g; Carbohydrate 75.5 g; Dietary Fibre 4.5 g; Cholesterol 104.5 mg; 2490 kJ (595 Cal)

COOK'S FILE
Note: Chinese roast duck can be bought from Asian barbecue food shops or restaurants.

1

2

3

CREAMY VEAL WITH MUSHROOMS

Preparation time: 15 minutes
Cooking time: 30 minutes
Serves 4

100 g butter
500 g veal schnitzel, cut into
    3 cm pieces
300 g Swiss brown mushrooms,
    sliced
3 cloves garlic, crushed
3/4 cup (185 ml) dry white wine
1/2 cup (125 ml) chicken stock
200 ml thick cream
1–2 tablespoons lemon juice
400 g pappardelle

1 Melt half the butter in a large frying pan over medium heat. Add the veal in batches and cook for 2–3 minutes, or until golden brown. Remove the veal from the pan and keep warm.

2 Add the remaining butter to the same pan and heat until foaming. Add the mushrooms and garlic and cook, stirring, over low heat for 5 minutes. Pour in the wine and stock, scraping the bottom of the pan with a wooden spoon, and simmer, covered, for 10 minutes. Remove the lid, add the cream and simmer for 5 minutes, or until the sauce thickens. Stir in the lemon juice, veal and any juices until warmed through. Season to taste. Meanwhile, cook the pasta in a large saucepan of boiling water until *al dente*. Toss the sauce through the pasta and serve immediately.

NUTRITION PER SERVE
Fat 40.5 g; Protein 45 g; Carbohydrate 74 g; Dietary Fibre 5 g; Cholesterol 235.5 mg; 3660 kJ (875 Cal)

PAPPARDELLE WITH FRESH SALMON AND GREMOLATA

Preparation time: 15 minutes
Cooking time: 15 minutes
Serves 4

½ cup (30 g) chopped fresh
  flat-leaf parsley
3 teaspoons grated lemon rind
2 cloves garlic, finely chopped
400 g pappardelle
¼ cup (60 ml) extra virgin olive oil
500 g fresh salmon fillet
2 teaspoons olive oil, extra

1   To make the gremolata, put the parsley, lemon rind and garlic in a bowl and mix together well. Cook the pasta in a large saucepan of boiling water until *al dente*. Drain, return to the pan, then add the olive oil and toss gently. Add the gremolata to the bowl with the pasta and toss again.

2   Remove the skin and any bones from the salmon. Heat the extra olive oil in a frying pan and cook the salmon over medium heat for 3–4 minutes, turning once during cooking. Take care not to overcook the fish. Flake the salmon into large pieces and toss through the pasta. Season to taste with salt and cracked black pepper, divide among four warm serving plates and serve.

NUTRITION PER SERVE
Fat 24.5 g; Protein 37.5 g; Carbohydrate 70.5 g; Dietary Fibre 3.5 g; Cholesterol 83 mg; 2755 kJ (660 Cal)

1

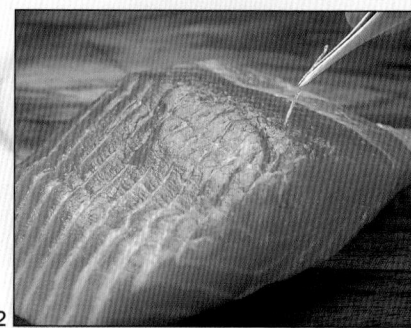

2

STRACCI WITH ARTICHOKES AND CHARGRILLED CHICKEN

Preparation time: 10 minutes
Cooking time: 20 minutes
Serves 6

1 tablespoon olive oil
3 chicken breast fillets
500 g stracci
8 slices prosciutto
280 g jar artichokes in oil, drained and quartered, oil reserved
150 g semi-dried tomatoes, thinly sliced
80 g baby rocket leaves
2–3 tablespoons balsamic vinegar

1 Lightly brush a chargrill or frying pan with the oil and heat over high heat. Cook the chicken for 6–8 minutes each side, or until cooked through. Cut into thin slices on the diagonal. Set aside.

2 Cook the pasta in a large saucepan of boiling water until *al dente*. Meanwhile, place the prosciutto on a lined grill tray and cook under a hot grill for 2 minutes each side, or until crisp. Cool slightly and break into pieces. Drain the pasta, then combine with the chicken, prosciutto, artichokes, tomato and rocket in a bowl and toss. Whisk together 1/4 cup (60 ml) of the reserved artichoke oil and the balsamic vinegar and toss through the pasta mixture. Season to taste with salt and cracked black pepper, then serve.

NUTRITION PER SERVE
Fat 9 g; Protein 30 g; Carbohydrate 51 g; Dietary Fibre 4 g; Cholesterol 103 mg; 1705 kJ (410 Cal)

SEAFOOD LASAGNE

Preparation time: 15 minutes
Cooking time: 15 minutes
Serves 4

1 tablespoon olive oil
2 cloves garlic, crushed
1/4 teaspoon saffron threads
600 g bottled tomato pasta sauce
750 g mixed raw seafood, cut into
 3 cm pieces (use scallops and
 peeled prawns or prepared
 marinara mix)
120 g English spinach
200 g fresh lasagne sheets (4 sheets),
 cut into twelve 10 cm x 16 cm
 rectangles

3/4 cup (165 g) mascarpone
3/4 cup (75 g) grated Parmesan

1 Heat the oil in a large saucepan, add the garlic, saffron and pasta sauce, reduce the heat and simmer for 8 minutes, or until it thickens slightly. Add the seafood and cook for 2 minutes, or until cooked, then season. Remove from the heat.

2 Blanch the spinach in a large saucepan of boiling water for 30 seconds. Remove with tongs, transfer to a colander and drain well. Cook the pasta in the same saucepan of boiling water for 1–2 minutes, or until *al dente*. Remove and arrange the sheets individually on a tray to prevent them sticking.

3 To assemble, lay a pasta rectangle on four ovenproof serving plates. Use half the mascarpone to spread over the pasta sheets. Top with half the spinach leaves and half the seafood sauce. Sprinkle with one third of the Parmesan. Repeat to give two layers, finishing with a third pasta sheet. Sprinkle with the remaining cheese. Place under a medium grill for 2 minutes, or until the cheese is slightly melted. Serve immediately.

NUTRITION PER SERVE
Fat 28.5 g; Protein 52.5 g; Carbohydrate 47 g; Dietary Fibre 5 g; Cholesterol 364 mg; 2750 kJ (655 Cal)

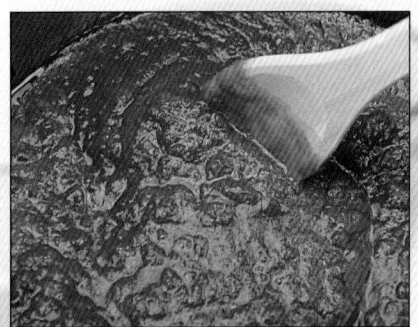

BEETROOT RAVIOLI WITH A SAGE BURNT BUTTER

Preparation time: 15 minutes
Cooking time: 10 minutes
Serves 4

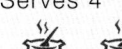

340 g jar baby beetroots in sweet
  vinegar
40 g grated Parmesan
250 g fresh ricotta
750 g fresh lasagne sheets (4 sheets)
fine cornmeal, for sprinkling
200 g butter, chopped
1/4 cup (5 g) fresh sage, torn
2 cloves garlic, crushed

1 Drain the beetroot, then grate it
into a bowl. Add the Parmesan and
ricotta and mix well. Lay a sheet of
pasta on a flat surface and place
evenly spaced tablespoons of the
ricotta mixture on the pasta to give
12 mounds—four across and three
down. Flatten the mounds of filling
slightly. Lightly brush the edges of
the pasta sheet and around each pile
of ricotta mix with water.

2 Place a second sheet of pasta over
the top and gently press around each
mound to seal and enclose the filling.
Using a pasta wheel or sharp knife,
cut the pasta into 12 ravioli. Lay
them out separately on a lined tray
that has been sprinkled with the
cornmeal. Repeat with the remaining
filling and lasagne sheets to make
24 ravioli. Gently remove any excess
air bubbles after cutting so that they
are completely sealed.

3 Cook the pasta in a large saucepan
of boiling water until *al dente*. Drain,
divide among four serving plates
and keep warm. Melt the butter in a
saucepan and cook for 3–4 minutes,
or until golden brown. Remove from
the heat, stir in the sage and garlic
and spoon over the ravioli. Sprinkle
with shaved Parmesan, if desired,
and season with pepper.

NUTRITION PER SERVE
Fat 52 g; Protein 15.5 g; Carbohydrate 32.5 g;
Dietary Fibre 3 g; Cholesterol 167.5 mg;
2720 kJ (650 Cal)

1

2

3

WARM PASTA AND SMOKED SALMON STACK

Preparation time: 15 minutes
Cooking time: 15 minutes
Serves 4

1.5 kg vine-ripened tomatoes
2 cloves garlic, crushed
1 teaspoon sugar
1/3 cup (80 ml) good-quality olive oil
3 tablespoons chopped fresh flat-leaf parsley
6 fresh lasagne sheets
400 g smoked salmon
100 g baby rocket leaves
extra virgin olive oil, for drizzling

1 Score a cross in the base of each tomato and place them in a bowl of boiling water for 1 minute. Plunge into cold water and peel the skin away from the cross. Remove the core, then transfer to a food processor or blender and, using the pulse button, process until roughly chopped. Transfer to a saucepan with the garlic and sugar, bring to the boil, then reduce the heat and simmer for 5 minutes, or until reduced slightly. Remove from the heat and gradually whisk in the oil. Stir in the parsley, and season. Keep warm.

2 Cut the lasagne sheets in half widthways to give 12 pieces, each about 12 cm squares. Cook the pasta in a large saucepan of boiling water in two batches until *al dente*. Remove from the water and lay out flat individually to prevent sticking. Place a pasta sheet on four plates. Set aside 1/3 cup of the tomato mix. Spoon half the remaining tomato mixture over the pasta sheets, then half the smoked salmon and rocket leaves. Repeat to give two layers. Finish with a third sheet of pasta. Top each pasta stack with a tablespoon of the tomato sauce, drizzle with a little extra virgin olive oil and serve immediately.

NUTRITION PER SERVE
Fat 24.5 g; Protein 32 g; Carbohydrate 36.5 g; Dietary Fibre 6.5 g; Cholesterol 48 mg; 2065 kJ (495 Cal)

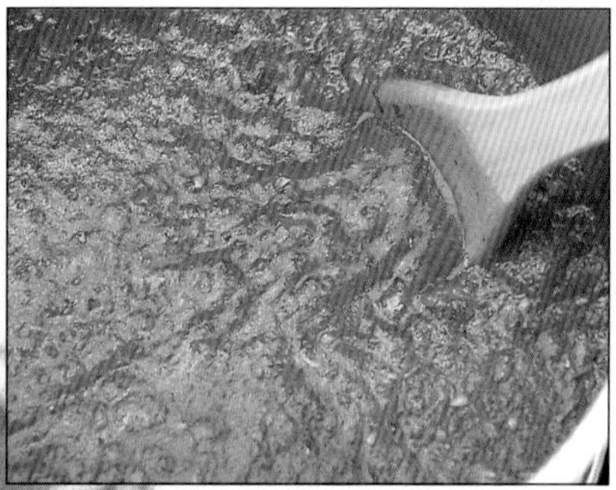

TUNA AND CHERMOULA ON PAPPARDELLE

Preparation time: 15 minutes +
  20 minutes marinating
Cooking time: 30 minutes
Serves 4

500 g sweet potato, cut into
  2 cm cubes
100 ml olive oil
2 cups (60 g) fresh coriander leaves,
  finely chopped
2 cups (40 g) fresh flat-leaf parsley,
  chopped
3 cloves garlic, crushed
3 teaspoons ground cumin
1/4 cup (60 ml) lemon juice
4 x 180 g tuna steaks
400 g pappardelle

1 Preheat the oven to moderately
hot 200°C (400°F/Gas 6). Toss the
sweet potato in 2 tablespoons of the
oil, place on a baking tray and roast
for 25–30 minutes, or until tender.
2 To make the chermoula, place the
coriander, parsley, garlic, cumin and
3/4 teaspoon cracked black pepper in
a small food processor and process
until a rough paste forms. Transfer to
a bowl and stir in the lemon juice
and 1 tablespoon of the oil. Place the
tuna in a non-metallic bowl, cover
with 2 tablespoons of the chermoula
and toss until it is evenly coated.
Marinate in the refrigerator for
20 minutes. Meanwhile, cook the
pasta in a large saucepan of boiling
water until *al dente*. Drain, return to
the pan and mix in the remaining
chermoula and oil. Keep warm.
3 Heat a lightly oiled chargrill pan
over high heat. Cook the tuna for
2 minutes each side, or until done
to your liking. Cut into 2 cm cubes,
toss through the pasta with the sweet
potato and serve.

NUTRITION PER SERVE
Fat 34 g; Protein 62 g; Carbohydrate 89.5 g;
Dietary Fibre 7 g; Cholesterol 83 mg;
3830 kJ (915 Cal)

QUICK MUSHROOM AND RICOTTA CANNELLONI

Preparation time: 15 minutes
Cooking time: 30 minutes
Serves 4

500 g button mushrooms
200 g fresh lasagne sheets
2 tablespoons olive oil
3 cloves garlic, crushed
2 tablespoons lemon juice
400 g fresh ricotta
3 tablespoons chopped fresh basil
425 g bottled tomato pasta sauce
1 cup (150 g) grated mozzarella
   cheese

1 Preheat the oven to moderate 180°C (350°F/Gas 4). Place the mushrooms in a food processor and pulse until finely chopped. Cut the lasagne sheets into twelve 13 cm x 16 cm rectangles.

2 Heat the oil in a large frying pan over medium heat. Add the garlic and chopped mushrooms and cook, stirring, for 3 minutes. Add the lemon juice and cook for a further 2 minutes, or until softened. Transfer the mushroom mixture to a sieve over a bowl to collect the juices, pressing with a spoon to remove as much moisture as possible. Reserve.

3 Place the mushrooms in a bowl with the ricotta and basil. Add plenty of salt and black pepper and mix well. Take a lasagne sheet and place heaped tablespoons of the mixture along one long edge. Roll up and place in a greased 2 litre 16 cm x 30 cm ovenproof ceramic dish. Repeat with the remaining mixture and lasagne sheets. It is preferable to have the cannelloni in a single layer. Pour on the reserved mushroom cooking liquid then pour on the pasta sauce. Sprinkle with cheese and bake for 25 minutes, or until golden and bubbling. Serve with salad.

NUTRITION PER SERVE
Fat 29.5 g; Protein 32.5 g; Carbohydrate 37.5 g; Dietary Fibre 6 g; Cholesterol 90 mg; 2290 kJ (545 Cal)

INDEX

INTERNATIONAL GLOSSARY OF INGREDIENTS

capsicum	red or green pepper	fresh coriander	fresh cilantro
eggplant	aubergine	tomato purée (Aus.)	sieved crushed tomatoes/ passata (UK)
tomato paste (Aus.)	tomato purée, double concentrate (UK)	zucchini	courgette

Published by Murdoch Books®, a division of Murdoch Magazines Pty Limited, GPO Box 1203, Sydney NSW 1045.

Managing Editor: Rachel Carter **Editor:** Zoë Harpham **Creative Director:** Marylouise Brammer **Designer:** Michelle Cutler **Food Director:** Jane Lawson **Food Editor:** Rebecca Clancy **Recipe Development:** Alison Adams, Ruth Armstrong, Rebecca Clancy, Ross Dobson, Michelle Earl, Jo Glynn, Fiona Hammond, Katy Holder, Kathy Knudsen, Jane Lawson, Michelle Lawton, Valli Little, Barbara Lowery, Kate Murdoch, Christine Osmond, Sally Parker, Wendy Quisumbing, Melita Smilovic, Angela Tregonning **Home Economists:** Justine Johnson, Valli Little, Evelyn Morris, Kate Murdoch, Kim Passenger, Angela Tregonning **Photographers:** Joe Filshie, Reg Morrison (steps) **Food Stylist:** Georgina Dolling **Food Preparation:** Justine Poole, Christine Sheppard (cover) **Nutritionist:** Dr Susanna Holt **Index:** Puddingburn Publishing Services **UK Consultant:** Maggi Altham **CEO & Publisher:** Anne Wilson.

The nutritional information provided for each recipe does not include garnishes or accompaniments, such as rice, unless they are included in specific quantities in the ingredients. The values are approximations and can be affected by biological and seasonal variations in food, the unknown composition of some manufactured foods and uncertainty in the dietary database. Nutrient data given are derived primarily from the NUTTAB95 database produced by the Australian New Zealand Food Authority.